THE MAGIC OF NETWORKING

Copyright © 2021 Travis Sims All rights reserved. "No part of this publication may be reproduced, distributed, or transmitted in any form or by any means, including photocopying, recording, or other electronic or mechanical methods, or by any information storage and retrieval system without the prior written permission of the publisher, except in the case of very brief quotations embodied in critical reviews and certain other noncommercial uses permitted by copyright law."

ACKNOWLEDGMENT

My first acknowledgment and thank you goes to my beautiful wife Dawn Sims. Thank you for believing in me and allowing me the space to be a creator. I am sure it is not always easy being married to an entrepreneurial spirit. You are by my side at every idea and every turn I make in the world. I'm thankful to have you as my co-pilot.

Thank you to the many people who have helped me learn and practice both the art and science of networking throughout my 16+ years' experience. I learn from every person I meet in a crowded networking event or on a Zoom meeting.

Additionally, my special thanks to Les Hill, my business coach who coached me into writing this entire book by video. Record just one video per week for your next book and use it as a video library that goes with the book. Priceless advice that made this project fun and profitable at the same time.

A special thanks to AGC Accelerated Global Connections members, a community of goal driven leaders in service to others. You have allowed me to share a presence in your business and life. Although I may be a speaker, teacher, trainer, or coach. I have great support from a network of people that come around to help one another when needed. You are truly the reason why I do what I do. I am consistently growing personally and professionally because of our great leaders in AGC.

DEDICATION

I would like to dedicate this book to my parents Dennis & Joy Sims. My parents gave me a real-life education in small business. They owned and operated a lawn care business while I was growing up.

I watched my dad work hard every day with and beside men half his age. Long after they went home for the day my dad would stay out in the garage and grease tractors and sharpen blades to get equipment ready for the next day. My mom would sit at the kitchen table and do payroll, send out invoices, and balance the books. I watched her work to manage expenses and save for the winter. Growing up I heard phrases like "You get what you work for." "It's not what you know, but who you know that makes the difference." "Word of mouth is the best advertising that you can do."

These life lessons molded me into the person and business leader that I would become. I have lived most my life as a hardworking, dream chasing, risk taking, entrepreneur, and small business owner. I've taken the lessons my parents taught me and went on to continuing my education in business and networking and I have dedicated my life to sharing and helping others in small business and entrepreneurship.

TABLE OF CONTENT

ACKNOWLEDGMENT	4
DEDICATION	6
INTRODUCTION	13
CHAPTER ONE	18
WHAT IS NETWORKING?	18
CHAPTER TWO	28
TYPES OF NETWORKING	28
CHAPTER THREE	36
THE CORE OF A GOOD NETWORK	36
CHAPTER FOUR	46
THE MAGIC OF NETWORKING	46
CHAPTER FIVE	60

BEST WAYS NETWORKING CAN BE DONE	60
CHAPTER SIX	68
THE INSTRUMENTAL IMPACT OF A GROWTH MINDSET IN NETWORKING	68
CHAPTER SEVEN	76
RELATIONSHIP BETWEEN BUSINESS SUCCESS AND NETWORKING	76
CHAPTER EIGHT	82
HOW TO NETWORK EFFICIENTLY	82
CHAPTER NINE	92
THE PRINCIPLES OF NETWORKING	92
CHAPTER TEN	110
SALES	110
CHAPTER ELEVEN	118
THE BENEFITS OF BUSINESS NETWORKING	118

CHAPTER TWELVE	124
THE MAGIC OF CONSISTENCY IN NETWORKING.	124
CHAPTER THIRTEEN	130
BUILDING TRUST	130
THE CULTURE OF NETWORKING	138
CHAPTER FIFTEEN	150
THE POWER OF TEAMWORK IN NETWORKING	150
CHAPTER SIXTEEN	156
REFERRALS	156
CHAPTER SEVENTEEN	162
NETWORKING UP	162
CHAPTER EIGHTEEN	170
DIVERSITY WITHIN YOUR NETWORK	170
CHAPTER NINETEEN	178

THE MAGICAL IMPACT OF
RELATIONSHIPS IN NETWORKING   178

CHAPTER TWENTY   190

ACCOUNTABILITY; THE SECRET OF
SUCCESS IN NETWORKING   190

AFTERWORDS   199

INTRODUCTION

Networking is not merely the exchange of information with others, and it is certainly not about begging for favors. Networking is about establishing and nurturing long-term, mutually beneficial relationships with the people you meet. Experts agree that the most connected people are often the most successful. When you invest in your relationships, personally and professionally, it can pay you back in dividends throughout the course of your career. Networking will help you develop and improve your skill set, stay on top of the latest trends in your industry, keep a pulse on the job market, meet prospective mentors, partners, and clients, and gain access to the necessary resources that will foster your career development.

Networking is used by professionals to widen their circles of connections, find out about job opportunities, and to increase their awareness of news and trends in their fields.

Business owners may network to develop relationships with people and companies they may do business with in the future. Professional networking platforms provide an online location for people to engage with other professionals, join groups, post blogs, and share information.

People generally join networking groups based on a single common point of interest that all members share.

It goes without saying that networking is incredibly important during a job search. Your chances of landing the job increase tenfold with the right employee referral. And, if you are looking to make a career change, your professional network can support you by helping you find connections in the industry you are trying to break into or helping you find leads for jobs at specific companies.

Take the time to build meaningful relationships with those in your professional circle, so when the time comes to search for work, you can tap into those valuable connections for referrals, insights into job leads, and other valuable information.

The importance of the saying "no man is an Island" has been proven to be the reason why many of us need to make a collective effort in the bid to achieve professional success. For many individuals that have succeeded in their career, the causes have largely been contributed to the strong networking channels they have created over time.

Whether you are a student, professional, or entrepreneur, networking is one of the most important things you can do to advance your career. It is an essential process that should be implemented throughout all stages of your professional journey.
There are different types of Networking. It is not a one-size fits all concept. Instead of choosing, you diversify as they suit your personality, schedule, and your needs. There are also various styles of Networking, which enables you to achieve your set goals.

Network has a great core that enables its efficiency, effectiveness, and excellent. In it we learn to develop trust, build relationships, connect authentically, create community, give referrals, have good teamwork, and work ethics. This core is the foundation of Networking successfully because by doing this, you align with its principles.

Now you are able to network successfully when you implement the best ways. There are immense benefits involved in networking. There are glaring effects in networking efficiently; it is shown in business and career success.

The magic of Networking is relished when you are consistent with it. It improves your business and helps to elevate your career. It shows you the importance of time management, the power of teamwork in networking, how to build a stable community and the importance of referrals.

Networking is great for this because entrepreneurs, business owners, and successful people who are themselves involved in networking are typically people who are pursuing excellence in their business and personal lives and are naturally positive and uplifting.

Finally, every intelligent person involved in business knows is important to invest in money, but only the wise also invest in relationships. These relationships are your network and your network is your net worth. Invest your most important assets, which is time on people, which can in turn bring out the best in you, personally and professionally. This network of people that share in our passions and values will become an interpersonal safety net that guarantees greater output and personal fulfillment in our careers and businesses.

SECTION ONE

NETWORKING

"Networking is not the question for business professionals, networking is the answer."

Travis Sims

CHAPTER ONE

WHAT IS NETWORKING?

Networking is all about establishing and nurturing a long term mutually beneficial relationship with the people you meet, no matter the place or circumstance. The beautiful thing in this is the opportunity to network daily and this is limitless.

Networking is utilized in developing contacts, the exchange of ideas among people with a common profession or special interest, usually in an informal social setting to further one's career. It often begins with a single point of common ground.

Networking is used by professionals to expand their circles of acquaintances to find out about job opportunities in their industries and to increase their awareness of the news and trends in their fields. It is not about selling yourself over to people for selfish gains, but it is all about building long term relationships as well as a good reputation over time. It involves meeting and getting to know people who can assist and who can potentially help you in return. Good networking jives with a good foundation of trust and support and all these takes time and commitment.

IS NETWORKING JUST THE NEXT BANDWAGON?
Networking is not everyone's cup of tea, to some it seems draining, time consuming and awkward on some occasions which greatly depend on your personality. When you have a workload of appointments to meet and a truckload of to-do list to cross, having a perceived small talk with a total stranger is the last thing on your mind as you are reminded of your tight schedule. Every other thing in life can be recovered apart from time, so who you spend it with and what you spend it for matters a great deal to you.

However, the strength a Professional network can have over your career success cannot be over emphasized especially when it is efficient and effective. An efficient and effective network with the right people can help you land that dream job faster and give you an enormous advantage throughout the stages of your career.

In life collective effort is needed to achieve professional success, as the saying goes "Effective Teamwork brings about the dream result". Individuals who have strong networks which they have created over time tend to have more success in their careers. Who you network with and their relevance to your career matters a lot but you will know if you do not try.

Success in a career is largely attributed to the multiple streams of ideas and information you receive. When networks have been created it nurtures avenues of ideas which can help to sustain long term relationships and mutual respect. The Greater the information and ideas you receive from your pool of networks the greater your career advancement. You can achieve greater heights when you have a strong and lasting network glued with good relationships with others. It is a key tool for growth in achieving a resourceful career and business.

Networking is one of the most important things you can do to advance your career. It is an essential process that should be adopted through all the stages of your professional career and business.
The goal of networking is not about connecting with as many people as possible, on the contrary it is about meeting those that can advance and endorse your skillset, show you opportunities and direct you to other well-connected people. It is not a competition and you do not garner points by amassing more communication with people, networking is much greater and better than that.

Do not assume that networking is an activity reserved for your time out of office and off the clock or just for leisure that is quite shortsighted to see networking that way. There is much more value in connecting and networking in the workplace and out of it no matter what your need may be, it is astonishingly beneficial to your career development.

MOTIVATION BEHIND NETWORKING

1. Bringing in a New business: With the opportunities provided to network with individuals in your industry, you can learn new ideas, innovations by brainstorming with intelligent minds, new opportunities arise, and you can see from a better perspective. You can then give birth to your best ideas which can be a new business.

2. Forming Strategic Alliances: The beauty in networking is that it gives birth to communities which result to strong and strategic alliances. Smart and like-minded individuals from all spheres of life connected together through the means of a network thanks to technology. Entrepreneurs, CEOs, Professionals can get together strategize and benefit mutually from one another.

3. Getting knowledge on new opportunities: There is an old adage that says without information you are deformed. Engaging in a community of serious likeminded people gives you the leverage to get beneficial information. Networking sites like LinkedIn is of tremendous help and other helpful social networks.

4. Exchanging ideas: Networking is a great opportunity to exchange best practice knowledge, learn about the business techniques of your peers and stay abreast of the latest industry developments. A wide network of informed, interconnected contacts means broader access to new and valuable information.

The opportunity to gather new information is an often-overlooked benefit of networking, as it is not the most obvious one, but it also offers career progression and development.

5. Getting access to novel marketing and distributing channels: It enables you to interact with potential interest groups, get opportunities for collaboration especially when the project is too big or complex to be done alone. Now if a project is complex, you will require all the help you need to achieve it, and that is achieved by teamwork. People come with new, different but innovative ideas that can solve problems.

In the same vein you get access to new and additional technology that can bring the best value in your career and all these are completely rooted in having a good and reliable network.

You will obtain knowledge on the latest and best business process as those in AGC Accelerated Global Connections are currently enjoying.

6. Career Growth: This should be your greatest motivation, connecting with professionals you may have met in Seminars, Workshops, Conferences and so on, networking at this point is of immense importance because this can advance your career or business. You can even develop mentors and teachers in your field that can help guide and mentor you. This will make you more efficient, effective, and excellent in all that you do.

7. Launching a new product: This is a great motivation for networking because you need all the help you can get. You alone at the beginning know the work you may have put into a new product and how good it is. You may need a recommendation from a well-respected person that is highly respected in the industry. A word of recommendation from this individual who is in a sphere of influence will make a remarkable progress in your product or the services you offer. Imagine Jeff Bezos recommending my book for Entrepreneurs, think about Elon Musk recommending a new product launched into the market.

I personally I have read books that were more expensive because of a recommendation or foreword by a well-known person I place in high esteem. Now the Entrepreneur is benefiting enormously from their network, because of those in their sphere of influence. If you have not started networking, you are running late already you must start now because you have been missing out on great opportunities, the benefits are ginormous. Gone are the days that is simply about what you know, what you know is great, but it should be heavily backed by who you know and how well they know you, this is very important.

8. Getting Access to Professionals, Business Owners etc: Having a good network broadens your opportunity to gain access to Professionals, CEOs who can do so much to improve your craft in so many ways. It gives you the opportunity to meet Interesting People. You never know who you may come across during networking events like conferences, meetups, and trade shows. It is an opportunity to meet influential people who could offer you your next job, career opportunity, or client. Some of them may be highly successful entrepreneurs or investors who may be on the lookout for the next big idea, and you may happen to show up at the right time, talk to them and pitch your idea to turn it into a reality. The opportunity to make high-profile connections is endless.

9. Establishing a brand name: Having a brand is what makes you stand out from the competition, attract clients, and get noticed. As you start networking, you start discovering different facets of your brand that connect with people. It helps you craft your story to use in your daily communication and social channels.

To build a formidable network, you must

- Build relationships
- Develop Trust
- Pass Referrals
- Share Business.

NETWORKING IS NOT JUST A TRENDY WORD

Networking did not just evolve yesterday, it is not a buzzword, a trendy word or just a fancy word, it has been the secret to success in every venture in life, career, in business, sports, religion, and politics.

Networking is not the question for business professionals, networking is the answer, it is the core in business in achieving excellent output you need the input of an excellent team. It helps to provide you the tools you require for progress.

The highest compliment you can give a business owner or salesperson is an introduction to your network. They get referrals, business deals and the right advice for building and career development like AGC (Accelerated Global Connections does. In a great network you can get the best help you need.

A lot is invested into networking, because you are building something very important and not with selfish ambitions. The beautiful thing involved is that a good network always finds a need to sort the desires of your heart. It could be some advice from a more experienced professional, it could be a connection to a financial opportunity a lot of people are unaware of, it could be referrals, and recommendations. The list is endless. As you invest into this beautiful process with your time, talent, and treasure you learn a lot of things that will never be taken away from you. You will see and enjoy the beauty of a community. You see how powerful and important a community can be and this can be achieved by getting involved in or building a good network. Now, are you going through it or you are growing through it? Food for thought!

Building a Network is not just a trendy word, as culture, is a way of life. A lot of people are successful in their careers and businesses just by investing into networking and the outcome has been remarkable. You cannot be a career minded person and networking is not in the picture, you cannot make it to the top in your niche.

You need to create a network before needing it, the reason for this is networking is basically about giving and helping others and through this means a good relationship can be formed. The person becomes a part of your network, when a business opportunity comes their way, he or she may be willingly to refer you if it aligns with your specialty and expertise.

Your transaction should not be about business alone, but it should be about relationships. Your transactions should and must be relational, in this a better relationship is formed, this gives for trust which is a very important building block of a good network.

Building a good network is key in building up your career and your business, because its importance to life is ginormous. Build your network with people, engage in the network, attend, update and connect with other members of your network. Engage in your network in your highest capacity. It is more beneficial to you than without it. Build meaningful relationships, develop trust, connect authentically not for self-centered reasons, foster the relationship in beautiful ways in your best ability. Cultivate the relationship, you see how plants are cultivated, it takes time to do the work and it takes a lot from all involved but when it starts to blossom it is evident for all to see and this takes time. It takes time to achieve trust, if you believe it will come overnight, it must be a really long night.

As you cultivate and nurture your network, a lot of shifting happens you tend to see a lot of things from a better perspective, but now with a different perspective you can see better in that area of your career because you are connected to intellectuals and like-minded people who can help you sharpen your skillset and make you more productive. Get answers to questions, top-notch advice that will benefit you tremendously.

In networking you should be leveraging technology, enhance it to build better relationships in business and in your career with like-minded people. We have a multitude of social media networks such as LinkedIn, Facebook, Twitter, Instagram, Clubhouse, etc. They look social, but a lot of businesses have made their mark through these platforms and they will continue to do so while you are still reading this book.

During this phase of building a good network you are getting better and creative, more innovative, and resourceful. You are better educated, and you are advancing better before you started networking in your business and in your career. Always remember the more you learn, the more you earn.

It is never too early or too late to invest in your network. The best way to improve is to get involved because networking should be at the core of your career, indeed no man is an island.

"Just give, do not even worry about the gain, it comes naturally."

Travis Sims

CHAPTER TWO

TYPES OF NETWORKING

There are 5 different types of Networking.

1. Closed Contact Networks
Organizations whose purpose is principally to help members exchange business referrals. Such groups in this type of network are called closed contact referral groups. It is a closed contact network because it is based on one person per profession or specialty. Most of these groups meet weekly, often in the early morning or during the lunch hour.

It helps to provide highly focused opportunities for you and your associates to begin developing your referral marketing campaigns. Since is a closed contact group the number businessmen or women and professionals are limited to small groups of people, but the beauty in this is that all the members will be carrying your business cards around with them everywhere they go. That is an astonishing act of referral. The net result is like having up to 50 salespeople working for you. With this immense benefit one will really have to invest a lot to have a solid great personal and professional relationship with their network.

You will have to meet the demands efficiently, effectively, and excellently or suffer removal from the group and will no longer gain the trust for referrals.

It is quite demanding just as the benefit is encouraging. Every member of the network is expected to have a schedule that will allow them to be in attendance to almost all their meetings. Regular attendance is essential to foster better relationships with

other members of the group and getting to know their businesses which is essential.
Great examples of such groups include Master Networks, BNI, LeTip, B2B, Goldstar etc.

2. Online/Social Media Networks
In this network, the use for social media is to build your brand and your credibility with the people you are connected to by providing value for your connections and followers. This is relatively inexpensive and not as demanding. It is not restricted and not bounded by attendance. It is an easy way to network and show your presence, that is, the presence of your product and the services you have to offer. You can offer to a wide range at the same time with unimaginable technology. It involves a lot of social outlet and opportunities to interact, build relationships, cultivate friendships that will definitely aid you. If people like you, they will patronize you just because they like you.

During a worldwide pandemic, every other type of network folded up shop at least physically, but the online and social media networks soared. Every other network depended on it to strive and survive for the meantime, while those in this network thrive. Business and transactions were done seamlessly from their comfort zone or rather lockdown zone. The Social Media was the niche by which all business thrived, its importance is beyond words and should be leveraged. Realistic Schedules were made for meetings, professionals and Business owners and workers worked effectively at home, lots of referrals were made, it became the clutch of every other network, it truly showed during that difficult time, that it is the type of network we cannot do without. Some examples include LinkedIn, Facebook, Instagram, Twitter, Clubhouse etc.

3. Professional Associations

This type of network is specific to their industry, members tend to be from one specific type of industry, such as health, architecture, accounting, banking, engineering etc.

The primary purpose of a professional association is to sharpen the saw, to exchange information, innovations, and ideas. They help you locate your target market; they send referrals, and such networks have an abundance mindset, meaning all they care about is helping you advance and grow.

They are centered on building meaningful professional connection and relationship. Those outside their circle are not welcome no matter what, they work with credentials.

4. Service Clubs Organizations

This network is focused on community, unlike more business-oriented groups, service groups, they are not set up primarily for referral networking; their activities are focused on service to the community.

They are centered on how they can give to the community, not to grow me, not on the receiving end but on the giving end. Although while giving time and effort to civic duties, they form lasting relationships that boosts and deepens their personal and business networks.

If you go in not to benefit but to contribute, the social capital you accrue will eventually reward you in other ways and from other directions not excluding business. Examples include Rotary, Lions, Kiwanis, Optimist etc.

5. Open Contact Organizations

It is open because it can permit more than one person per profession unlike closed contacts. These are general business groups that allows many people from various different and the same professions assemble and network together. Various Realtors, Financial Advisors, Insurance, Mortgage Reps, etc.

They may also hold events where guest speakers present on important business topics or to discuss issues concerning all spheres of life. A great benefit of this network is that they offer participants an opportunity to make valuable contacts with many other businesspeople in the network. You are able to meet a lot of people, there is enough business for everyone. You can collaborate with people who are in the same association with you.

There are great ways for referrals and opportunities to find the right company or people you can do business with. If the people like you, they will like what you do. The open contact organizations are the best networks. Examples include Accelerated Global Connections (AGC), Chamber of Commerce, Network After Work, First Thursday, etc.

The biggest question will be which of these networks I should choose; the answer is not to choose but rather diversify. I recommend choosing three out of the five types of networks that fits your style. Even as is important, as it is that you know the types of networks, it is also important to know the styles of networking.

THE STYLES OF NETWORKING

There are 3 styles of networking.

1. Do it yourself (DIY) Networking: People networking in this case tend to do everything by themselves without requesting of help or assistance from outside the group. You will find a lot of these on Meetup. They are often FREE and you certainly get what you pay for. It is an island concept and because of this it is characterized by the following. They are:

- Unorganized
- Often unprofessional
- No support rendered
- Small footprints
- Small results.

2. Do it or Else (DIE) Networking: In this style of networking, people tend to respond to instructions, attendance to meetings are mandatory, every performance from you is graded, there are lots of limitations, you are told what to do at every given time, there are lots of restrictions, it is demanding and works with a scarcity mindset, they are often group focused, with small amounts of people with a small footprint getting small results.

3. Do It Together (DIT): This is the best networking style as far networking is concerned. A Network has always been about teamwork and you need the right style of networking to achieve a good Network.

They operate with an abundance mindset, always willing and ready to help and assist others. There is freedom of choice for attendance and activity. The social environment or atmosphere is great and at its very best. Great relationships are built, referrals happen faster, leaders and those of much higher status can be reached easily and by faster means, they are reachable and approachable, no hidden fees, everything is transparent. They have big footprints and big results.

It proves to show that networking is about helping others. This style teaches one to stop selling and start building meaningful relationship that will be rooted in trust.

It may be of great surprise to you that Network differs from networking. Networking is a means by which you interact with people, now when the networking is done effectively, efficiently and excellently, then a network is formed. Networking is the means, the Network is the people, this is the community that helps, advance and make you better personally and professionally.

"Networking is a relationship sport."

Travis Sims

CHAPTER THREE

THE CORE OF A GOOD NETWORK

Networking is the means by which a Network is achieved. A good type and style of Networking will give room to a great network.

For this chapter we will accessing the core that makes a great network. Every formidable entity has a core, a backbone and this is what makes it stand no matter the storms and turbulence that comes at it, it will always stand strong no matter what.

1. To Develop Trust: This is very important aspect of networking. Most of the people you now network with today you are not related to them by blood, marriage, or adoption. You met them physically or virtually and took a chance with them or they took a chance with you as the case may be.

The Network is deemed successful when it is embedded in trust. Trust is a valuable asset that you have, it is priceless to you, you do not just toss it to whoever smiles at you or whoever says the word hello. Trust is earned and this happens overtime. It takes a lot of time to get that approval, you develop it, nurture it, build it and this takes patience, integrity, and excellence on your part.

People tend to be connected to people that are trustworthy and can take their word to the bank, because your yes is a yes and your no is a no. No compromise, no double talk, you are not two-faced. When you say i will meet you up by 7am, 7am you are there, not 7:01am and give excuses about traffic and so on. People take you by your words and most importantly by your actions, your words must align with your actions and that's integrity.

People will want to be connected with, do business and refer the people they can trust. For most of the time when you have met up with expectations, that will place you on good grounds and high standing. I will not be willing for to include you in my circle of business partners and associates when you are untrustworthy and unreliable. You do not meet up with deals when due, filled with excuses or nonchalance, you go around with wrong mindset and poor work ethics. People network with, do business with, and refer only the individuals they can trust. If you can be trusted in excellence, efficiency, and effectiveness, you are good to go.

2. Building Relationships: This is beautiful backbone of a good network. When some people think about networking in business, the only thing they can see is dollar bills, but that is not the right way to go. You must build a good relationship with the people you are networking with the goal is never to sell yourself, far from it, when you think about networking what comes to mind is building relationships. You are open to help the people you are network with when they are in need.

A good network consists of people you have built, established, and nurtured a long term mutually beneficial relationship with, not a salesperson mentality that all you think about is, what is it for me. The me-me-me mentality, laced with selfish gains alone. In your network if everyone is taking who will be giving? If everyone wants to sell who then will want to buy.

It takes time to build a relationship, no part of it is by-passed, when you have a shallow relationship, it will not stand the test of time. But a firmly rooted relationship which has enjoyed a lot of investment, will definitely stand the test of time.

When your relationship becomes well-built, we can be seen not just as a partner, not just a friend but as a family. This at the end of the day can impact greatly and positively your career and business in an unbelievable fashion.

A relationship that is business based alone will achieve nothing concrete, but you want the relationship to be transactional and you want to have a deeply rooted relationship with the client, you must be open, share your ideas, make it as clear as day to your supposed client.

You also must instill an abundance mindset; with this mentality you will have a great network. Be open to give business tips, trendy and better methods of doing things in your industry. It proves that you want the persons in your network to excel, even if they cannot directly buy from you. You can make recommendations and referrals; this can mean a lot to your network and it will be duly appreciated.

3. New Connections: This is also important in networking, the more connected you are the higher your chances of being successful in your industry. You can only make new connections by getting started, speak more to the people you meet, you cannot just attend an event where you meet fellow professionals, business owners and just walk away without engaging in any meaningful discussion; you can start up with a compliment of one's outfit, Introduce yourself, give a business card, talk a little about yourself and show genuine will to know about the other person, you have no idea who you may be sitting next to you.

I know we have different personalities, some may say " I do not speak with strangers" or "I am introverted". For the case of the those introverted, you can memorize words before an outing, take the position of the person you will be speaking with, look at the mirror and give your trial, the more you try you will get better, as they say, "practice makes perfect". For those that find it difficult to speak to strangers, you can start by; saying something, talk about the weather, sports, politics, or the trendy topic in town and you may be surprised at the turn out, keep it in mind that the goal is that you are genuine in your intention in knowing the person.

Is great to put emphasis on the others but this equally starts from here because without beginning a connection with someone, you cannot develop trust, you cannot build relationships, it all starts from here.

You may say it is risky, what if it doesn't turn out well, you must know that the greatest in every field and sphere of life took a risk. They left their comfort zone, those that stay too comfortable in their comfort zones never got their dream result. No matter what happens you must know that on the other side of your biggest fear is your biggest awakening. The victory that you seek just lies on the other side of what frightens you, but you will have gave to go for it. Even if there is a setback, know that every setback is a path to your comeback.

You never can tell the result of the relationship you are trying to build just by having a new connection, you do not only have to think outside the box but must move outside the box. Move outside of your network of just family, friends, colleagues, members of my religious group, people I meet at the gym and meet new people outside this sphere of your regular routine. The results of the outcome can be tremendous.

4. Connect Authentically: This is also a building block of a good network. You as an individual must strive to connect to the people you meet authentically. No sales pitch, the people you meet and connect with must know and believe that you are genuine and your goal in meeting them is to bring things that are beneficial and productive to them. Not to use them and see them as your steppingstones to wonderland.

When all these can be accomplished then your core becomes solid. By now you have built a foundation that you are a reliable and trustworthy person, that you are worthy of their time and their commitment.

You can also now have the opportunity to build a better and deeper relationship with them, this is very important. Most Entrepreneurs have time only for first impressions and when they believe in your authenticity, then you are good to go. A lot of individuals have gotten great clients and this is worthy of note.

5. Referrals: This is an important core of having a good network for individuals who desire to have a great network with his or her client. Referrals are great to build a great relationship with your network which can help to build your career and business. As you continue to receive referrals, it is great to prove that you care about their progress and the bond that holds the network together. It improves the career and business of your partner, what your referrals and recommendations can do is unimaginable. The power of referrals is what control great trade in the world today. Its importance can never be overlooked.

6. Create community: Creating community is everything as far networking is concerned. We have different personalities in all kinds of professions, careers, and business in a unit together like a family. Ready to give tremendous help to every member of the community as the needs arise. In your community of networks, referrals and recommendations are made for your benefit.

Community is built and rooted in trust, where there is already a healthy and functional working relationship that has been built over time. This is where the connections make major impact and give the big break.

The magnificence of your network is based on the community of professionals you have. Always remember your net worth is directly proportional to your network.

7. Teamwork: This is the bond that holds the biggest, strongest, and greatest network, business, association, the list is endless. Without teamwork nothing big can be achieved, nothing phenomenal can be achieved and this is not rocket science because you cannot do it alone, indeed no one is an island.

A Network thrives where there is great teamwork, this concept is as old as human life itself, it can never be overemphasized, inspiring feats can never be achieved when you decide to it alone.

When everyone in the network plays their roles efficiently, effectively, and excellently the outcome will be nothing short of phenomenal. Everyone in the network must always be reminded about their importance and denote that without their efficient, fully focused and committed performance nothing outside the ordinary can be achieved.

For example, the human body is a good example to show the importance of teamwork in a network. The human body is a network of so many parts and they must work in sync to achieve health and proper functionality and when this is achieved excellently, effectively and excellently the body is at ease, a state of health. But when the body is in disarray, here comes disease and it never ends well. No matter the size of the body part, whether the hands, arms, eyes, nose etc. They should play their roles properly in outmost cooperation, then the best is seen and achieved.

8. A Good Work Ethic: For a network to be great, everyone involved must pull their weight, they must roll their sleeves up and get to work. For anything to thrive the importance of a good work ethic can never be underestimated. It is a great resource everyone in your network should bring to the table to make things work in unbelievable fashion.

Members in a network must consciously and actively bring their 'A' game to it because this is great business. The input you put into it, is the output you see. Things do not just happen on their own, people make it work. You must get it done, if you do not like what you see you need to get a lot done using the right principle, the right methodology and process then you can see the right results.

Diligence must be put into it, great determination, and discipline, these are what constitute a great work ethic.

Sometimes you may be busy as we live life in a busy world, everyone is busy with one thing or the other, one must be diligent enough to draw out strategic schedule that can work perfectly for everyone to have a fruitful network.

This principle explained above works for everything as far as this world is concerned, it is not far-fetched, it just works the way Mother Nature has designed it function. Teamwork in networking is of immense importance.

9. Friendship: This is the icing on the cake. It is not of out of place that friendship is a core in having a network. Networking works seamlessly when you are friends with your network. It will bring better yield when you are already in a cordial relationship with your network. It begets better relationships, and we all know that better relationships equal a better network.

Friendship is a great fortress in networking, the circle just gets better, and you can delight in the opportunities in having a community.

Now before an individual, colleague, partner can be your friend, it means it did not happen out of the blue. Relationships are built over time, trust have been formed overtime. There have been multiple meaningful connections in time past.

You can give a good assessment of the identity of your friends, You are fully aware of their strength and weaknesses. You know their biggest motivation.

The popular saying will always call our attention that says, "Show me your friend and I will tell you who you are." This is your inner circle, your friends will and should be the first in your list of the members in your network which forms your community.

From the very beginning while meeting the client for the first time, the goal is to build a great relationship and you have no idea the impact they will make in your business and career.

"Become a Victor and not a Victim."

Travis Sims

CHAPTER FOUR

THE MAGIC OF NETWORKING

It is not breaking news that the most connected people are often the most successful people.

When you invest in your relationships whether they are personnel or professional using the core of a network such as developing trust, creating new connections, good work ethic, connecting authentically.

It rewards you in ways you cannot imagine during your career. Whether you are a professional, or entrepreneur, networking is one of the most important things you can do to advance your career. It is an essential process that you should implement throughout all stages of your professional journey. Networking is not about connecting with as many people as possible. It is about meeting the ones who can endorse your skillsets, show you great opportunities and direct you to other, well-connected people. Indeed, networking is magical.

The following are the benefits of networking.

1. Networking Helps You To Improve Your Skillset
In your current field of practice as a professional or in business as a Business Owner or an employee, networking tends to improve and sharpen your skills. A great development is made when you meet other great professionals or business owners in your field who have been there before you and have been very successful in their niche by a great standard, the responsibility is on you to learn from their greatness. Now when these people are

in your network, in enables you to improve. You are taught best by them; they show you the way to go around in your career and be successful.

Your expertise becomes better, you now tend to organize affairs in a better way than before you met them. It improves your creative alertness and accelerates your creative intelligence. You start seeing things from a better view and great ideas tends to pop up.

2. Keeps You In Flow In The Job Market

Networking tends to help you to keep in touch about the trends and the current happenings in the job market and the business world entirely. It opens new doors of opportunities you could have missed but just because you engage in a productive and professional network you see the magic in it.

Expanding your contacts can open doors to new opportunities for business, career advancement, personal growth, or simply new knowledge. Active networking helps to keep you top of mind when opportunities such as job opportunities arise and increases your likelihood of receiving introductions to potentially relevant people or even a referral.

Do not forget that many jobs do not even get advertised – particularly as your career advances – so being a recognized part of networks is a key way to gain access to opportunities that you might not have otherwise.

Professional networking opens many doors in the form of career advice, lasting relationships and even landing your dream role. You never know who might be hiring for your ideal job, or know someone who is, and the more people you have in your network, the likelier you are to be the first to know when those big job opportunities come up.

A LinkedIn study found that 80% of professionals consider networking important for their career success. One of the main reasons for this is the different opportunities that you discover through networking, which you would have otherwise never seen or thought of before.

The business world of today runs on connecting the right people with each other, and for a reason. Networking could bring you in touch with someone who has insider information about a job that has not yet been advertised. That one meeting you have could change the course of your career. This benefit cannot be overemphasized. Great importance lies in getting to know the right and important information especially for the search of a better job or career change.

3. It Helps You To Meet Prospective Clients And Partners
This is another wonderful benefit in networking. When a network is effective, efficient, and excellent you have tons of clients and partners ready to do business with you especially when you have history of a great track records. Referrals and recommendations play a magical role here.

4. You Get To Help Others
Here comes the abundance mindset, the acts of service rarely go unrecognized, especially when they have a big impact in a community. Assisting someone else with their career goals can be truly rewarding. Through networking, you can connect with people who need your expertise and knowledge and help other professionals overcome career obstacles. This is a great way to expand and diversify your network and become more noticeable within your sector. In some cases, you may also have the opportunity to exchange services with other companies - a win-win scenario.

5. You Gain Access To The Best Resources
Networking helps you gain ground and a good access to not just the available resources but also the best, right there you the get

one in the inside watching out for you and guiding you correctly. You have great links to the powers that be, even if not directly, indirectly: if it gets to the required destination. You may not directly know the Big Guys at the table but because of your network, you may be connected to a person in your network that plays golf with the Big Guys which in return can elevate your career development immensely.

6. It Serves As An Extra Resource Library
This plays a major role as you plan to advance and get better in your career and business. This is of tremendous assistance because no one is MR, Miss or Mrs. Know-it-all.

Have a good network that links you to other professionals in your field. During the good period of effective communication, you tend to learn a lot and this can give you the access to make requests to know more it than area. You may even get it for free based on your relationship with the individual. He or she may just be willingly to give back as a good sign of the abundance mindset, which is a benefit of having a great network.

A lot of persons would like to come to your rescue, both in your field and in other fields in case you also want to diversify. As you are new in the area where you have diversified, you can get all the help and assistance that you require. It also enables you to have access to updated information that can be relevant to you and your business. This extra resource will produce magical effects in your career.

This is one the biggest advantages of networking, it helps to provide the opportunity to meet interesting people from various professions and sectors. This allows you to gain insights into the commonalities between different professions and later apply knowledge from one area to another – also known as 'transference knowledge'. It helps you to successfully connect with new and different people. This can potentially lead to a job, referrals, or introductions, but it can also lead to interesting conversations, new friendships, and learning opportunities.

Treat networking as a knowledge exchange process to actively learn about industries' latest developments, which could eventually help you in your career. It enables you to be able to see things from a different perspective.

It is a good idea to actively ask your contacts about developments and techniques, but also to keep an eye on what kinds of articles your contacts are sharing on LinkedIn, do not forget to comment to let them know that you have appreciated the piece. And do not discount the insights of people from other industries – they may be able to offer new angles you have not previously considered.

7. You Can Find New Mentors

When you are just starting in your career and are still new to the industry, you may need some guidance. Networking facilitates the opportunity to find and connect with people who have experience in your field, and that could act as mentors to you. Having people, you can talk to during times of need and ask for guidance is an invaluable asset to your professional growth.

As long as you have a strong network of professional connections, you can be confident that someone within your sphere will be able to answer even your toughest questions. And, if there is no definitive answer, you will have a solid sounding board to bounce ideas off and put into action step-by-step plans to tackle bigger problems.

8. You Can Gain Support From High Profile Individuals

Everyone wants to be connected and associated with the Big Wigs in your chosen career path and a support from them especially publicly is of tremendous help to elevate your career.

These persons can produce good recommendations, referrals, provide links on how to get the job, or just general advice that have benefited them before. This can help to raise your self-confidence and cause a positive growth in your status.

9. Growth In Your Status

Networking can help to bring about growth in your status from the helps, referrals, and recommendations you have benefited from. In time past you must have elevated your status and increase your profile in the business world.

When achievements have been made from your work, especially when you got a booking from a leading company, it makes you highly sought after and with these feathers in your hat, your profile became better than before, and this is good for business. The main point here is that networking placed you on the right track to start with and now with great determination, diligence, discipline in your part, you have made it to the top and great recognition can come from this.

Being visible and getting noticed is a benefit of networking that is essential in career building. Regularly attending professional and social events will help make you well known.

Create value for other attendees by listening carefully, following up on conversations, remembering names, and offering your knowledge and expertise.

You can then help to build your reputation as being a knowledgeable, reliable, and supportive member of your profession by offering useful information or tips to people who need it.

Raising your profile within professional circles will also help you stand out to recruiters, who are always on the lookout for strong talent and who may be more likely to approach you with their offers

10. It Results In Long-lasting Professional Relationships

It is not surprising that having a large network can bring you in contact with like-minded people who share similar interests, passions, and goals as you. These long-lasting contacts may be essential to your career progression and could help you climb the professional ladder. Often, these professional relationships can last a lifetime and can even develop into friendships.

11. Growth In Self Confidence

Networking helps you to become self-confidence, it may not really be an issue for the extroverted but for the introvert it may be a serious issue but as they continue to connect authentically, build bonds and connections with one another it increases the confidence level of the person.

By continually putting yourself out there and meeting new people, you are effectively stepping outside your comfort zone and building invaluable social skills and self-confidence that you can take with you anywhere. The more you network, the more you will grow and learn how to make lasting connections.

Every individual has their different personalities and temperament, but with a good open and state form of networking, they get better, they get along, feel valued and the narrative will now showcase a better tale. The more you involve in networking, the more confident you will become.

The more people you meet, the more you step outside your comfort zone and build invaluable social skills and self-confidence. You can use these skills throughout your professional life.

By putting yourself out there, you are gaining self-confidence by interacting with people.

Acquiring social skills is a must for business, and it also boosts self-confidence'. When you start your networking journey, you may need to experiment with different strategies to make yourself sound interesting to others. This will put your self-confidence to the test. But, as you continue networking, you sharpen different facets of your skillset, and there is an overall boost to your confidence that you can utilize in different aspects of your life.

12. It Gets You Noticed

There are many talented professionals out there. It is crucial that you are visible amongst the crowd and make opportunities come to you instead of the other way around. One way to do this is through networking. When you start building relationships and foster conversations about the value you can bring to an organization, word starts spreading. Before you know it, you become that one person who 'knows everyone' and people want to connect with you for all sorts of opportunities.

13. You Are Accessible To Career Advice And Support

Receiving advice from experienced peers is an important benefit of networking, especially if your contact has already gone through a similar journey, you are about to undertake. You have the opportunity to discuss common challenges and get immediate feedback and solutions for them. That said, it is not just about receiving advice; networking is also about offering assistance to others when they reach out to you. The more you give, the stronger the quality of your network.

Gaining the advice of experienced peers is an important benefit of networking. Discussing common challenges and opportunities opens the door to valuable suggestions and guidance. Offering genuine assistance to your contacts also sets a strong foundation for receiving support in return when you need it

14. It Shines a Light On Your Offerings

Networking is a fantastic opportunity for individuals, especially entrepreneurs, to get in front of other professionals that may be interested in learning about what you do and your start-up's offerings. Making these connections can provide endless benefits for entrepreneurs.' Building lasting professional connections with people allows you to highlight your credibility, earn others' trust and demonstrate your professional value. This can result in word-of-mouth marketing that leads to new opportunities, such as entrepreneurs and business owners offering their services or signing up as long-term clients.

15. It Helps You Polish Your Elevator Pitch

An elevator pitch is a short description of something delivered in a quick, understandable format. People use it to pitch an idea for a company or product or to explain a job opportunity to others. This is relevant to networking events since most people do not have time for 10-minute-long introductions. Usually, you get less than a minute to convey your experience, interests, and passion to others and make yourself sound interesting. Using an effective elevator pitch can make another person want to form a lasting professional connection with you. Therefore, to make every meeting and conversation count, you need to craft a compelling elevator pitch.

16. It Gives You a Reality Check

When you are working in the same job for several years, it is easy to lose touch with how your skillset and experience translate to the outside world. Once you start connecting with other professionals, you can get a reality check of how other people within similar positions go on to have more successful careers. This is called upward comparison. This psychology theory suggests that comparing yourself to people you consider to be better than you motivates you to achieve similar success.

17. It Improves Your Mental Health
Developing good relationships can have positive effects on your mental and physical health. Indeed, Social connection is the greatest predictor of long-term happiness and the greatest long-term predictor of success. Through networking, you can develop a sense of camaraderie, worthiness, and purpose by connecting with individuals who share the same passions as you.

A professional network can assist your career in many ways, whether it is finding a job, securing a promotion, starting a business, or finding new clients. However, to achieve that, you need to step outside your comfort zone and start connecting with other people in your field. But remember, you cannot just build relationships; you need to maintain them too by regularly following up with your connections, whether it is a quick chit-chat at the annual industry conference or drinks at the weekly (virtual) happy hour.

18. Strengthen Business and Career Connections
Networking plays a major role in helping you to give your business and career a strong backing and it also enables it to get rooted in the business world. By having a good network, it means you now have good connections. Your connections to the right persons can strengthen your business and your career immensely. You advance in your career as you continue to get good recommendations from people that matters in the society. You now have a good reputation among wide range of people. You can now be connected to the industry leaders in your field.

Networking is about sharing, not taking. It is about forming trust and helping one another toward goals. Regularly engaging with your contacts and finding opportunities to assist them helps to strengthen the relationship. By doing this, you sow the seeds for reciprocal assistance when you need help to achieve your goals.

19. It Improves Your Communication Skills

Networking forces you to talk to strangers. It gives you a chance to effectively communicate your value to others and explain how and why you stand out from the crowd. Essentially, you are practicing your soft skills in real-time. The more you practice, the better you become at delivering your message with precision and clarity. This benefit is even more important for introverts who want to advance in their career.

20. Career Advancement

This is very important; networking helps to create a path that can take you to the top seamlessly as long as you have a good work ethic. You can work your socks off to get things done, you meet deadlines. You achieve great things in your field, networking may be that ray of light you need to bring you to the limelight.

Being visible and getting noticed is a benefit of networking that is essential in career building. Regularly attending professional and social events will help to get your well known. You can then help to build your reputation as being knowledgeable, reliable and supportive by offering useful information or tips to people who need it.

Your career is advanced, and networking puts a lot of work into career building. Not everyone is at the peak of their careers but as you have a good network and you are efficient, effective and excellent in your dealings with your clients and partners, your career will advance, courtesy the magic of networking.

21. It Enables You To Get Fresh Ideas

Your network can be an excellent source of new perspectives and ideas to help you in your role. Exchanging information on challenges, experiences and goals is a key benefit of networking because it allows you to gain new insights that you may not have otherwise thought of.

Far from it being a nuisance, most people love being asked for help. It is flattering and makes them feel useful. If you are struggling with a decision, challenge, or new direction, calling up a trusted former colleague, mentor, teacher or friend to organize a coffee can be beneficial to both of you, as they will in turn think of you when next they have a challenge.

It's easy to get caught up in the day-to-day of your professional realm and end up in a rut. By talking to others in your field or people with expertise in a particular area, you can gain insights that only come from viewing a situation with fresh eyes. Asking for opinions from contacts you trust or admire can help you see things in a new light and overcome roadblocks that you might not have known how to circumvent otherwise.

Offering helpful ideas in return is an excellent way to build your reputation as an innovative thinker.

22. Develop A Long-Lasting Relationship
The point of networking is to develop and nurture professional relationships, but some of the strongest and most long-standing friendships are born from work connections. Your networking contacts are probably like-minded people with similar goals as your own, so it is not unlikely that your professional support network will spill over into your personal friendships.

"Find the success in your failure."

Travis Sims

CHAPTER FIVE

BEST WAYS NETWORKING CAN BE DONE

Networking can be demanding at times, some label it to be pushy and overbearing but developing a wealth of contacts is invaluable to your career and the business your company generates.
Networking is a two-way street; it is a way of getting to know someone better and finding ways they might be able to help you and how you can help them in return.

A professional networking event is a great opportunity to present yourself, make new connections and even find yourself a new job. Current research shows that a large number of jobs are filled through networking. Successful networkers display a sincere interest in their networking contacts and work hard to develop a relationship, establish their credibility, and share their information and knowledge. To become a successful networker, you should follow the belief that everyone has something to learn and gain.

Networking is an ongoing process, it requires persistence, attention, organization and good will. Incorporate the art of networking into your job search and you will gain opportunities and build relationships that will last a lifetime. Demonstrate your value to potential clients and employers by knowing the best ways networking can be done.

1. Always Prepare
Fail to plan and you plan to fail. If you are hosting the event, make sure you have all the necessary materials ready, such as

name badges, business cards and brochures about your business. If you are attending an external networking event, make sure you have something to hold all the business cards you collect. If you get flustered when talking to people, try to rehearse what you will say beforehand this can also work well for introverts. Think about how you present yourself and your skills on LinkedIn and then consider that networking is the real life equivalent. Your delivery should be as polished and professional as your online version.

2. Meet People Through Other People

The best and easiest way to meet people is through referrals. Stick around with the people you already know and who know the people you are looking to meet. Being introduced through them or joining in with their conversations you will very likely receive a warm welcome and introduction to the person you wanted an introduction to. This is a similar effect to LinkedIn through their online introduction tool, or even through joining the right circle at an event with somebody you know.

3. There Should Be A Target

A networking event is not a social gathering – you are there to achieve something. Set yourself a goal, such as the number of people you want to talk to or be introduced to. If the number is 20 or 30 people, you must ensure that you leave with 20 or 30 business cards.

4. Don't Have A Set Agenda

Networking is not asking everyone you know for a job, in fact, when you network you should never ask someone for a job. You should ask people for information that will assist you in your job search. Your main networking goal should be to build a relationship and establish rapport so when a potential opportunity may arise in the future, your contact may be willing to refer you.

Remember: networking is about developing relationships, so do not try to close a deal. You are not there to do business; you are there to meet valuable contacts. Your only agenda should be a set number of people to talk to and your objective is to get their business cards and potentially do business with them in the future. So avoid any sales pitches or business propositions.

5. Use Your Resume as a Tool for Advice
Another easy yet highly effective way to network during a job search is to ask others who you have established a relationship with to review your resume and give you feedback on how to improve it. Using this technique is valuable for a number of reasons. When reviewing your resume, they will discover your work history, your previous titles, your objectives, and many things they may not yet know about you. They may remember a company or a connection that your background may be perfectly suited to.

6. Be A Good Guest
If you are attending a networking event it is important to be a good guest. Make sure you are not complacent and avoid sitting in the corner by yourself which never works well, otherwise nobody will talk to you. If you do not make the effort to work the room you will miss out on great opportunities that can advance your career . Be nice, friendly and open when you speak to people, and if you see someone sitting alone, go and say hello.

7. Talk and Listen
When networking, be sure that you do not do all the talking. The key to being a good conversationalist is being a good listener. If you have asked another person for advice or their opinion, make sure they have the opportunity to offer it and tell you. Or perhaps they are looking for you to add value to their work. If you do all the talking, the person may feel you are uninterested in what they have to say and unsure what action to take with the information you have supplied.

You must talk to people, but you must also listen to what the other person is saying. Otherwise, you will not know whether that person is the right person for you to be talking to and connecting with. Nobody likes a talkative person that never listens. Ask yourself: "do I really need this person's business card or does he or she have nothing to do with my objective?" Listen and you will learn.

8. Give Referrals
From the backdrop of talking and listening, if you get the impression that the person you are talking to is not relevant to your business, but you know of someone else at the event that may be of interest to them, you can refer them to the other person. This will help you to make good business connections as your contacts will remember you as the referrer; this is the abundance mindset that plays a major role in networking.

9. Share A Success Story
Once you have found a topic the other person may be interested in and you can offer advice on it, present a solution by telling a story about how you helped others in a similar situation. Tell them about the problem and how you solved it, but keep it short and sweet. Start by telling them about the problem and then your solution. Include lots of information on how disastrous things were before it came to a happy ending, where everything worked out for the better.

10. Ask For Suggestions on How to Expand Your Network
One of the main goals of networking is not only to meet one or two people, but also to tap into the network of the people you are meeting with. Each separate person you meet will know approximately another 250 people, and if you can gain introductions to some of these contacts, you will quickly increase your network and your chances of finding an extremely valuable connection. Ask your contacts if they can recommend a

professional organization or the names of some of the people you should be talking with.

11. Leverage Social Media
Social media is an effective way to get to know important contacts better and without the pressure of a face-to-face meeting that you may not be prepared for. Seek out like-minded or key contacts you would like to know better within your LinkedIn profile, Facebook, Twitter and more. Try commenting on a link they post or responding to a comment they make, start a conversation with them and offer them value in return. When you have the opportunity to meet them in person it will be easier to reference previous communications with them.

12. Take Two Business Cards
At networking events there is a lot of exchanging of business cards – when talking to someone, ask for two business cards. Do not just take one for yourself, but also take one for someone you may know who may be interested in their business.

13. Time Management
Before you start networking, be sure to have an agenda and keep the meeting on track. Time is money and people are never happy with someone that takes up too much of their time. By planning your meeting ahead of time, you establish your professionalism, you gain credibility and cover all the critical topics you wanted to cover.

It is important to keep track of time at networking events. If it is a breakfast seminar, then you will only have about 30 to 45 minutes to network and if you have given yourself the goal of talking to 10 people that gives you about three to four minutes with each person. So make sure to manage your time effectively, do not spend 20 minutes talking to someone you already know or have met at a previous networking event, but rather invest that time in talking to new people and this will bring great result at the end of the day.

14. Write Everything Down

If you do not have a great memory, keep a pen and paper in your pocket and write everything down. If you are going to meet 10 people in an hour you cannot guarantee yourself that, you will remember the finer details of your conversation with each person, so it is best to keep a written record of who you have spoken to and their line of business, along with a few details to jog your memory.

15. Follow Up

This is a very important aspect in the field, if you want to establish rapport with another person, create a reason to keep the relationship going. If you read an article that adds to a discussion you had during a networking meeting, save it and send it to them with a brief note on what you found interesting and how you think it could benefit them. Try and find at least two or three opportunities yearly to reconnect with the members of your network.

Follow up with your newly formed contact the next day and remind them of what your business has to offer to gauge their interest. If you do not follow up with your new contacts within one to two days, you have just wasted the entire networking event which can leave a wrong mark on you.

16. Always Remember To Say Thank You

Building a network is about creating a genuine, caring relationship. Thank your connection for the information they have given and see if you can help them in any way. Share any knowledge you feel would be useful for them. Keep notes on what you learn about your contacts so your future correspondence can have a personalized touch.

17. Online Presence
Ensure your online profile is always up to date. Recruiters often use social media platforms to probe potential candidates, and even to check out your skills and experience. These few basic rules will help you succeed at networking. Remember, the goal at networking is to build relationships and networks. A good, reliable network can result in new customers, partners and opportunities. Get out there and meet people, but ensure you are following these networking tips to make sure you are meeting people in the right way.

"Breakthroughs never happen while you are comfortable."

Travis Sims

CHAPTER SIX

THE INSTRUMENTAL IMPACT OF A GROWTH MINDSET IN NETWORKING

A mindset is a set of assumptions, methods, or notions held by one or more people or groups of people. A mindset can also be seen as arising out of a person's worldview or philosophy of life. It is someone's way of thinking and their opinions.

It is your collection of thoughts and beliefs that shape your thought habits. Your thought habits affect how you think, what you feel, and what you do. It impacts how you make sense of the world, and how you make sense of you. Your mindset is a big deal.

In Networking, having a growth mindset is very important; it has an efficient, effective, and excellent impact on networking.

There are 2 major types of Mindset

1. Fixed Mindset.
2. Growth Mindset.

Features Of A Fixed Mindset

-They Give Up Easily
People with a fixed mindset tend to give up easily when they encounter obstacles or challenges but instead of embracing them, they give up. They do not like to put in the effort, they do not want to go through the burn to achieve success. When they face challenges, they will just throw in the towel and say I am done.

They have made up their mind that anything stressful for them is not worth it, hence they have this kind of mindset.

-They Have A Predetermined Potential
They have a mediocre mentality, they just say this is all I want to be, and this is who I want to be, they do not strive for excellence. There is no way for them to improve.

- Failure Is The Limit Of Their Abilities And Intelligence It Is Just The Start Of It
For example, they say I am 50years old and I too old to learn anything or to make an impact. They always give excuses because of their challenges. They have the mindset that they are too late already and there is no room for growth or to learn anything new.

-They Avoid Challenges
Challenges come to make you better when you overcome them. A person who has a fixed mindset wants to avoid them by not facing them because they just find a way that, they will never be successful doing it. They have a negative mentality regarding challenges. They see challenges as what has come to destroy them, so they run from it completely.

-They Like To Stick With What They Know And They Do Not Want To Learn Anything New
They just like to stick with what they already know. They are not innovative; they do not have the desire to learn something new. They do not like new ideas, they do not want any out of the box approach. They just prefer the stereotypical lifestyle they are used to.

Instead of them wanting to learn something new, all they see is the difficulty in it. They are lost in the illusion of feeling that they are just fine with what that they already know.

Sticking with what you know is not a bad idea, but it becomes wrong when you are not open minded, you are not open to new ideas and innovations.

-They Take Feedback And Criticism Personally
They take criticism to the max and it is offensive to them even if the criticism is a constructive one. They do not want to be corrected no matter the manner or how the correction is done. While Networking one must be open to criticism that helps to build you up and make you a better person.

-They Have The I Will Never Improve Mindset
They just like to live in the status quo. They do only the minimum; they make no advancement in the things of life. They have a lazy mindset that they are either good at it or they are not, without making sufficient effort to improve.
They always conclude that the do not have any opportunity to do anything new than what they are currently doing. They see no point in trying anything new.

Features Of A Growth Mindset

-They Want To Try New Things
Those with a growth mindset always want to try new things. They try their hands on learning something new. No matter what it is they put up with the challenge to do better by learning new things.
They have the mentality that they can do whatever they want to do, and this starts by trying to do new things, things they have not done before.

There are a lot of platforms where they can learn new things from and can be innovative with them. The platforms include Google, YouTube etc.

Before we were once limited to what we know but now with the advancement of technology, you can access a lot of how-to's; how to network efficiently, how to bake a cake, how to prepare a special meal, how to get good clients for my business, how to respond in an interview, the list is endless. You have the opportunity to learn what you want to learn.

-They See Failures As An Opportunity And Growth
This is a lesson on your path to success. A person with a growth mindset does not put much emphasis on how many times he or she failed but how many times they pick themselves up and continued the journey.

People with a growth mindset see failure from a different perspective. You only truly failed when you stopped trying. When it did not work out as planned, your job is to go back to the drawing board, strategize, and come up with better plans than the ones that were previously used.

Thomas Edison an American inventor and Businessman once said
"I have not failed; I have just found ten thousand ways that will not work."

This indeed is an elite mentality, no wonder he is described as the greatest inventor in America History. With such Growth Mindset, no one should be surprised.

-Their Intelligence Can Be Developed
The more you learn new things, the better you become. This helps to sharpen your skills; it enhances your intelligence. This is very important in networking, because you know better now, you can do things easily, faster, and better. Development in your intelligence changes everything.

-They Embrace Obstacles, They Are Ready To Face Challenges

People with a growth mindset embrace obstacles; they see it as an opportunity to shine. They welcome the obstacle and see it as an avenue to learn something new, add to their wealth of experience and become better as a result.

Whenever they see a challenge on the way, they welcome it as another opportunity, and they embrace it.
Obstacles may cause you to change your plans, tweak some areas but those with a growth mindset will never abandon their goals.

-They Are Inspired By Other People's Success

When you see people excelling and are successful in what they do, you are inspired by it. Their success motivates you to do the same or even better. It challenges you to improve yourself and get better in every area that concerns you. This causes an immense amount of growth in your mindset.

Instead of being jealous and looking for an excuse to exempt yourself, instead you are motivated to improve and give a better performance. Improve on your work ethic, more than ever.

-They See Mistakes As A Channel To Growth

You figure out a better way of doing things in the process just like in the quote of Thomas Edison. You address the mistake and get new methods and plans so you can become better. It may sound difficult that you see mistake as a channel to growth, but it will be beneficial to you at the end of the day. Sometimes things are difficult, but it is worth it because you learn a lesson or two from it.

-They Find A Way To Be Happy

Even if it is a time of difficulty, people with a growth mindset are always positive. In a struggle they find a way to remain positive and know surely that everything will be alright. They face issues from that vantage point, so the situation on ground does not cloud their judgement, instead they can see from a better perspective without any form of anxiety. It is great to always remain positive no matter what.

There are other types of mindsets. For example, we have Positive mindset and Negative mindset. We also have Optimistic mindset and Pessimistic mindset. But in all the most important type relating to networking is the Fixed and Growth mindset.

A great quote from the late Civil Right Activist, Nobel Prize Award Winner, and Former President of South Africa, Nelson Mandela

"Do not judge me by my successes, judge me by how many times I fell down and got back up again."
This is from a man who had a growth mindset, and his impact stands the test of time.

Difference Between A Fixed and Growth Mindset
To identity whether you have a fixed mindset or a growth mindset, it shows how you are able to handle:

1. Challenges
Fixed Mindset:
-They avoid challenges at all costs.
-They treat challenges like a roadblock.
-They see challenges as a confrontation, and they avoid it as much as possible.

Growth Mindset:
-They embrace the challenges that come their way because they see it as an opportunity for growth.
- They do not allow challenges to get in their way. There is no roadblock with them.
- They confront challenges.

2. Obstacles
Fixed Mindset
-They give up easily. When it is not convenient, they throw in the towel.
Growth Mindset
- They persist through it no matter what.

3. Effort
Fixed Mindset
- They see effort as fruitless. They believe is not worth it.

Growth Mindset
- They see effort as an opportunity to master it. They master the situation through the effort they put in. They believe that what you put in is what you get out of it. They believe it is worth every part of it.

4. Criticism
Fixed Mindset
-They avoid criticism even when it is constructive.

Growth Mindset
-They see constructive criticism as a foundation to build from, where to grow from, and where to improve from. They like to engage in positive conservations.

5. Success Of Others
Fixed Mindset
-They are threatened by the success of others. It leads to jealousy and hate.

Growth Mindset
-They are encouraged, motivated, and inspired by the success of others. This helps to result in better performance.

"Are you going through it or are you growing through it?"

Travis Sims

CHAPTER SEVEN

RELATIONSHIP BETWEEN BUSINESS SUCCESS AND NETWORKING

Networking and Business success fits like hand and gloves, they will always go together. The world we live in today is like a global, you can reach out to everyone in the world without barriers, not even a geographic boundary can stop the influence of a good network.
Nowadays a large part of success in the business is tied to networking. The better your network the more efficient and effective your business with be. You will be linked so many persons around the globe as a result of this and your business will thrive.

Every intelligent person involved in business knows to invest in money, but only the wise also invest in relationships. How much time do we spend thinking about, planning for, and executing actions regarding financial investments? We work to balance our assets and liabilities and dream about stock options and retirement, but how often do we invest in our most valuable assets - people?

The ability to build a network of authentic personal and professional relationships, not your financial capital, is the most important asset you can have. It also involves your ability to work with other people who share the same passions and values. This network of people will become an interpersonal safety net that guarantees greater output and personal fulfillment.

A well-coordinated Business and its network yields the following:

Positive Influences
The people with whom you associate and spend time with influence who you are and what you become. Therefore, it is important to surround yourself with positive, uplifting people that help you to grow and thrive as a business owner and as a person. Positive people naturally exude their best attributes; these are the individuals with whom you want to associate and connect with.

Networking is great for this because entrepreneurs, business owners, and successful people who are themselves involved in networking are typically people who are pursuing excellence in their business and personal lives and are naturally positive and uplifting. You cannot help but receive a charge just from being in their presence. The knowledge you may gain is important, but the mindset you can adopt from them is invaluable.

Enhanced Knowledge
Networking builds your knowledge power, and not just through gaining insider information on the latest big deal. Having like-minded business owners and entrepreneurs with whom you can confer gives you the opportunity to learn and obtain advice from them on any conceivable topic related to your business and obtaining that important work-life balance. Family and business in this culture is inexorably entwined, so maintaining good family and business relationships are top in everyone's mind.

Better Business Opportunities
Powerful networks mean powerful position and business opportunities. More and more in today's business world, leaders prefer to become intermingled in important transactions with people they trust. Relationships establish and fortify that trust. That is why serious serial entrepreneurs, influencers, deal makers and multiple project players choose to seek out exclusive business networking opportunities.

Very often, networking provides opportunities for advanced training, conferences, and mentoring relationships that you may otherwise miss. A recommendation from a top entrepreneur or business owner for a conference or learning pathway can point you to knowledge of incalculable value.

Growing Confidence
Regularly participating in the right network and pushing yourself to engage with people you do not know, will help to increase your confidence. This is vitally important as a business owner or entrepreneur because your business growth depends on talking to the right people and forging lasting connections. If you are not very confident, networking is a great pathway to gaining the confidence you need for success. Pushing yourself to connect with others and being accepted into a network alongside them is a great confidence booster. As you become a part of the group, opening in conversations, and creating lasting connections with people further enhance your confidence.

Personal Satisfaction
In addition to the business-related benefits of networking, the personal satisfaction you can gain from contributing to the growth and opportunity of others is often the great reward. Networking can and should provide altruistic opportunities as well as business rewards. These may come through connections with other network partners who serve in non-profit causes or through the casual or structured mentoring of others.

Mentoring
Mentoring is an important aspect of networking. For Business to thrive mentoring must be involved and will handy when you belong to a well-seasoned network, it brings up all the possibilities and benefits in mentoring and its association with business.

Mentoring plays a great role in achieving success in business, it gives you the opportunity to stand on the shoulders of those before you, it enables you to not to the mistakes your mentors made, and this is a great edge in Business.

Virtually everyone has gained value from a mentoring relationship, either formally or informally. Bill Gates often refers to his ongoing relationship with Warren Buffett as a mentor. Facebook Founder Mark Zuckerberg counted Apple Founder Steve Jobs as a key mentor.

If you have learned any lessons about life and business, you have something to pass on to others. Healthy people have both inlets where people invest in them, and outlets where they themselves invest in other people. The Dead Sea is dead because it has inlets but no outlet. To thrive as successful people, we need to be receiving quality and pouring quality into others around us. This is a defining virtue of networking.

Networking is a superb way to tap into advice and expertise that you would not otherwise be able to obtain. Solid advice from the right person can sometimes be a critical factor in business and personal success. That knowledge can come through intense conversations, dinner meetings, or even casual discussions of mutual interest.

Increased Status
Networking can enable your business to be visible and seen and this can help to grow and improve your business in great ways. Now because of your good network of resourceful personalities in your network, whom you are networking with, it improves your status and that of business, it is even powerful enough to make it highly sorted after when you do your homework properly, by bringing the right product or service to the market, now with great endorsements, recommendations and referrals businesses will soar.

Being visible and getting seen is a benefit of networking that is vital in building and growing your career and business. More than this, being visible and getting seen in tandem with the right people can also mean an increase in your own standing among peers and others in your industry. "It is not what you know, but who you know and how well they know you" is true in business around the world. If you want a successful business, then you need to have a great source of relevant connections in your network that you can call on when you need them.

Networking can help to build your reputation as a knowledgeable, reliable, and supportive person who can provide useful information and connections to people who need it. You are also more likely to get more leads and referrals as you will be the one that pops into their head when they need what you offer. The right network can put you into contact with high quality, trusted, and powerful connections throughout numerous business and professional communities.

Business Connections
Networking provides you with a great source of connections and opens the door to highly influential people that can be a boon for your business. Often, just having a networking relationship with certain people enhances your standing and credibility, which therefore helps your business in numerous ways. And that influential person will already have a network you can tap into as well.

"On the other side of you biggest fear is your biggest awakening."

Travis Sims

CHAPTER EIGHT

HOW TO NETWORK EFFICIENTLY

The Magic of Networking is achieved when is done efficiently, effectively, and excellently. There are ways to network efficiently which can bring about the desired result.
The following are ways to network efficiently:

Use Your Resources
It has become easier to maintain a professional network due to technology. The internet is a valuable resource for creating, cultivating and communicating with your contacts. Use social media platforms to reach out to professionals in your area, to reconnect with old friends and to start a conversation with the people you meet while on the job. Sending a friend request or a brief message to a new contact may help them remember you and encourage them to seek out a mutual relationship.

Look For The Right People
Reach out to the people who can provide you with the specific help you need. If you are interested in a different field, connect with friends or family members who work in that industry. If you hope to switch to a new department in your workplace, talk to your colleagues who are a part of that team. You never know who might be able to help you at a later date, so make sure to connect with people working in a variety of industries and positions.

First, to find a networking event, you can check LinkedIn, which has an events section listed right on your personal homepage. There you can find happenings near you in a field you're interested in, Eventbrite also offers a similar service.

Once you have settled on an event, do your homework. You can check out who is attending by following the hashtag thread on social media to see who is posting about the event, reaching out to the organizer in advance, and sometimes the invitation platform (e.g., Eventbrite, Paperless Post) will share the RSVP list (without contact info). When you know the attendees, identify who you might have synergy with and who could be particularly helpful to your business or career.

Seek Out Networking Events
Socializing in person is still your best chance of creating a successful network. Attending company mixers, corporate retreats or community events will expose you to a variety of important contacts. Most likely, others at the events will also be networking and will be happy to exchange business cards or contact information. Be aware of your company's social calendar, your alma mater's reunion schedule and your community's social scene to find promising events.

Be Proactive
Cultivating your network year-round is crucial to maintaining beneficial connections. If you suddenly message a friend you have not spoken to since high school, they may not want to recommend you to their employer. Maintaining pleasant relationships with your extended network at all times is very important, even just by sending a short email to say hello, is the best way to make sure they are willing to help when you need them.

Know How To Give And Take
It is important to keep track of what the different contacts in your network can offer you. You will need to remember which of your previous co-workers now works in finance or which started teaching philosophy. Equally important is to know what you have to offer as a contact. Ideally, networking should be mutually beneficial, so be sure to let your network know how you can help

them. If you are willing to support your friends, they are more likely to return the favor.

Reach Out To People From Your Past
This is very important when we in networking mode not place all our focus in the here and now and also in the future by forgetting those that helped us in times past perhaps their efforts helped us to where we are now. But reconnecting with old bosses, mentors, co-worker and former coaches is key. They are likely in a different place in their careers and have made new connections that you can also tap into.

Contact Your Alumni Network
Speaking of your past, do not forget about your alumni organization. Most alumni networks have events and volunteer activities that are perfect for expanding your sphere of influence.

Try Giving A Compliment As An Ice-Breaker
Is great you begin your conversation with a compliment, it brings about your intended Client attention positively, everyone loves to be told something nice ab themselves. For example, "If there is something immediately noticeable about the person then feel free to shine that positivity on them by saying 'I love your jacket, I had to come over and find out where you got it,' that is a good way to start a conversation. Always try to be the person who raises the energy of other people around you.

Other valuable tips? Hold your drink in your left hand to leave your right available for shaking. Also, ask an open-ended question that engages meaningful conversation (e.g., what brings you here tonight as opposed to starting with what do you do), and on your way home, jot down a few notes about your conversation with each of the people you connected with to facilitate your follow up.

Always Follow Up
Truly networking events can be incredibly overstimulating. It is easy to get lost in the clutter, and rarely do you get the kind of quality time with someone at an event that will make a lasting impression. That is why the follow up after the event is more beneficial, it brings about better connection and helps you stay in touch.

If you have had a great exchange, ask the person the best way to stay in touch. Some people like email or phone; others prefer Facebook, Instagram, or LinkedIn. It will be great to send a text within 48 hours of the event to show you are interested and available and reference something you discussed so that your contact remembers you, this style is quite effective. In your follow up email, remind the person of a memorable moment of your conversation so they can quickly recall your exchange. Tell them what it was that stood out for you about them and give them that compliment, this aspect is very important.

Approach the follow up with a specific insight or ask to show you are both mindful and respectful of that person's time, "Never send an I would like to join your network" or "will you be my mentor" note, as it lacks the action-oriented drive that will make you stand out." Instead, propose a next step, e.g., invite them to meet again.

Join Hobby Groups
Professional organizations are a given. It is very important to join groups that share personal passions For example, by joining a book club, You will immediately have a common interest and connect with people on a real level.

An easy way to do this is by looking on Meetup.com, which is one of the world's largest network of local groups. Simply search your interest (e.g., knitting) in your location. Or, a simple Google search like "poetry clubs in Manhattan," will also yield useful results. Even joining a gym can be a way to meet people if you're into fitness.

Consider Starting A Podcast
A podcast will elevate your online presence, says Manning, thus making it easier for people to find you. Websites like Anchor allow you to record, and edit a podcast on your phone, for free. They'll even help you to secure sponsors.

Additionally, podcast hosts are always looking for other experts to share their insights. Often a host will invite you to contribute to their platform with the agreement you will allow them to be featured on yours. "This is a great way to increase your network and build a community," adds Manning. "When creating content, make sure that you are developing it for a specific target in mind. You want your platforms to specific to your field and provide value to all those involved."

Be Strategically Active On LinkedIn
"Spend 20 minutes in your day liking and commenting on colleagues' posts," says Toner. "Also try to share relevant articles and news at least once a week This keeps you popping up in searches and top of mind when people are perusing the site."

THE OPPORTUNITIES IN NETWORKING

1. Networking In The Workplace
One of the most obvious places to grow your network is in your workplace. Connections like these can provide you with referrals, job leads, mentoring and practical training. If you dedicate time and effort to getting to know your colleagues, they have the potential to help you advance in your current career or aid in the transition to a new one. Supervisors can write letters of recommendation; managers can give you inside information on

an opening in another department and previous coworkers can refer you to their new employer.

Your workplace network can also help you improve as a professional and as an employee. A mentor who is willing to give you advice and guidance can help you gain maturity and experience. A coworker who has a specific technical skill might be willing to offer you training. These opportunities for self-improvement in the workplace can make you a more valuable employee and a more attractive candidate for future job searches.

Seeking out opportunities to expand your workplace network is as easy as starting a conversation in the break room. Reach out to your coworkers and find out their professional history, their role in the company and their career goals. Getting to know them gives you information about both how they can help you and how you may be able to benefit them.

2. Networking For Career Development
Career development is essentially a map of your career journey. It begins with your education and ends when you retire. Career development includes the skills you acquired from your formal and informal education, the experience you gained at your first job and advancement opportunities you have in your current position. Networking is one of the most effective methods for accelerating the pace of your career development and providing you with new opportunities to succeed.

Your employer may provide you with official opportunities for career development, like training courses, seminars, or certification exams. However, most of the responsibility for developing professionally falls on you. There are several ways you can use your professional network for career development.

Career development is crucial for those seeking to grow professionally and using your network can be a valuable tool. Try to identify those in your network who may be able to provide you with new skills and experiences. Staying in touch with contacts who work in a wide variety of fields and at a variety of levels can help you become a more informed and capable professional. If you stay connected and involved, you never know when an exciting development opportunity might present itself.

3. Networking While Job Searching
The most common time for using your network is during a job search since many positions are filled using personal contacts instead of advertisements. If you are looking for a new career, your network is almost certainly your most powerful tool. Your network can provide you with job leads, reference letters, job search advice and insight into new fields. So, before you start emailing your resume to strangers, you should start by sharing it with some of your most promising contacts.

One of the best methods for using your network while job searching is social media. If you share the fact that you are looking for work with your social circles on your online professional profile and other sites, chances are that someone on your contact list is aware of an open position. The possibilities for using your network to job search are broad. For example, you might send your resume to a specific contact who works in the field you are interested in or to a colleague who has connections in a different state.

Although you might not anticipate an upcoming career change, it is still a good idea to maintain your network consistently. You never know when you might need to find a new position quickly, and close relationships with your contacts could be your best chance for a successful career change. If you regularly invest time and effort into your professional network, you will be able to draw on its resources when you need them.

SECTION TWO

PRINCIPLES OF NETWORKING

"On the other side of your current struggle is your next victory."

Travis Sims

CHAPTER NINE

THE PRINCIPLES OF NETWORKING

These are the fundamentals in networking. It is the very essence of having a good network. They form the basis of networking and this is what makes it tick.

The following are the principles of networking:

1. Integrity
Integrity is the practice of being honest and showing a consistent and uncompromising adherence to strong moral and ethical principles and values. It is regarded as the honesty and truthfulness or accuracy of one's actions. It stands in opposition to hypocrisy.
Integrity is the quality of having strong ethical principles that are followed at all times. Honesty and trust are central to integrity, as is consistency.

A person with integrity demonstrates sound moral and ethical principles and does the right thing, no matter who is watching. Integrity is the foundation on which a good network is built, it is a valuable principle a Person sees before they can network with you.
To have integrity means that a person is self-aware, accountable, responsible, truthful, trustworthy, reliable, they lead by example and that their actions are internally consistent. A person who has integrity can be trusted by coworkers, customers, and stakeholders etc.

People who demonstrate integrity draw others to them because they are trustworthy and dependable, and this attribute is very important for networking. As Associates, they are principled, and you can count on them to behave honorably.

Integrity is a valuable skill in a person because it indicates they will perform to the best of their ability and act on their principles. People will only do business with the people they can trust, people who are taking responsibility, truthful and reliable and this is a principle in networking that counts a lot.

When you have integrity, it simply means you are a person of your word and this brings about good reputation because words can easily spread. When you do not have integrity, people see you as a hypocrite and no one wants to be connected with you and even more to do business with you. Integrity emits a lot of confidence for those around you and this is attractive for good business.

2. Goal And Plan Setting
Goal setting involves the development of an action plan designed in order to motivate and guide a person or group toward a goal. It can be guided by goal-setting criteria (or rules) such as SMART criteria. Goal setting is a major component of personal and professional development.

Every goal should be specific; you must have in mind what achieve and not anything less. If in your network you desire to have 50 professionals in the network, then you should place as your goal and work towards it, definitely challenges will come but when the goal is your focus, you have to keep pressing on till the required outcome is achieved.

Every goal must be measurable, in your involvement in the network; your success so far should and can be measured. This gives the motivation to know if are on the right path.

Your goal must be attainable and realistic, so you should not bring up unrealistic expectations, because this can hugely cause disappointment and frustration. Work with what is achievable, and you improve steadily when your plans are achieved and also learn not to settle for less, your goal in networking must be realistic and at the same time, achievable.

Goals are timely, this helps to put you in tune and you must know that there is a time to begin and also time to end. You must be an effective and efficient time manager. When the goals and plans is time bound, it allows to place things as priority, work with a scale of preference, from this perspective you can work on and separate matters that are important from those that are not relevant to your goals and plans.

It has been proven that more specific and ambitious goals lead to more performance improvement than easy or general goals. Specific goals lead to significantly higher performance than general goals, no goals, or even the setting of an abstract goal such as urging people to do their best.

Holding ability constant, and given that there is goal commitment, the higher the goal the higher the performance. Variables such as praise, feedback, or the participation of people in decision-making about the goal only influence behavior to the extent that they lead to the setting of and subsequent commitment to a specific goal.

People perform better when they are committed to achieving certain goals. Through an understanding of the effect of goal setting on individual performance, organizations are able to use goal setting to benefit networking performance.

There is great importance of the expected outcomes of goal attainment.

Goals focus attention toward goal-relevant activities and away from goal-irrelevant activities. It serves as an energizer; higher goals induce greater effort, while low goals induce lesser effort. It also promotes persistence; constraints with regard to resources affect work pace.

Going into work with having a great plan in networking is daydream and also having great goals and plans without implementation is a nightmare. Both work hand-in-hand to achieve excellent results.

3. Win/Win Situations Produce Strong Connections
Having a strong network is extremely valuable because of the long-term impact it can have on your business. The relationships that you are building today may benefit you for years to come. That being said, if the relationship is going to have that long-term impact there must be a win/win situation where both parties benefit.

In the world of web design, having a professional network is often desired because of the possibility for getting referrals. Let us look at two potential scenarios to illustrate why win/win situations are important. In the first scenario there is an experienced web developer who does not do any design work. You are a designer, and you met this developer recently. You've received a few referrals from this developer, but you have not sent any clients his way because you already have another developer friend that you refer clients to.

In the second scenario we'll look at a potential relationship between a freelance designer (you) and a design agency. Your work on client projects tends to be with small businesses, blog designs, and other projects that you can handle on your own. From time-to-time you get inquiries from potential clients that are looking for help with a large project that is beyond the scope of something that you would handle on your own. You refer these people to a friend who runs a design agency that has a team of designers and developers and is better equipped to do an effective job on larger projects. In return, the agency sends you a fee for every referral you send their way that results in a paying client.

In the first scenario there is no win/win situation. The developer is sending referrals to you, so you are getting something out of it, but there's nothing in it for him because you already have an established relationship with another developer. The developer will eventually stop sending referrals to you if there is nothing in it for him, since he can find a better situation with another designer.

In the second scenario there is a definite win/win situation. You are sending quality referrals to the agency and when they result in business you are getting paid for those referrals. Unlike the first scenario, this one is likely to last because both parties' benefit.

When it comes to networking, many designers concentrate on what they can do to get referrals, without giving much thought to what they can offer others. In truly effective networking situations, there will always be some benefit for both parties. It may be referrals, money, services, advice and help, introductions to others, or just about anything that may be desirable.

When you are working on building your own network make sure that you understand the importance of finding win/win situations and look for opportunities to build these types of relationships. A good place to start is to examine the connections that you already have. Approaching these people will be much more effective than reaching out to someone that you have never had any contact with. Look at the people that you already know. How could you help them, and is there a way that they could give something back to you as well?

4. Give More Than You Get (Helping Others)

You must know that the abundance plays a great role in networking. So many people approach networking as a way to help their career, but often times they do not consider what they could be doing to help others. In general, if you are willing to help others, in some way they are likely to return the favor when the opportunity arrives. It is like the old saying, 'what goes around comes around."

You can do well to focus on getting to know more about the people already in your network. Look for ways that you can do something to help them, without focusing on what you will get in return. Those who are genuinely helpful to others will be appreciated and will likely benefit greatly from their network.

It is critical to remember that networking is a two-way street. Many people that want to build their network are only motivated by what they can get out of their network, rather than focusing on how they can help others.

There is nothing wrong with wanting to get something positive for yourself out of your networking efforts, but it is important to take an approach that will also benefit others in your network.

People who look for ways to help others will also benefit themselves because many people will repay the gesture at some point. We like to help people that have helped us, and this can be a powerful factor in networking.

When you want to strengthen a relationship with someone in your network, and connect for the first time with someone, think about ways that you could help them.

5. Activity Beats Inactivity

There will be times when others reach out to you and great opportunities fall in your lap (especially if you are more established) but in general it is a good practice to be proactive in your networking. Do not sit around and wait for others to approach you, make an effort to initiate contact and get to know someone.

Networking can come in various way, Facebook, LinkedIn, Twitter and other social networking sites are popular hangouts for Professionals. Email is also a great way to connect. More traditional face-to-face networking with those in your local area or at professional conferences and events is also highly effective. Whatever your approach, be proactive and do not leave your networking to chance.

6. Prioritize Quality Over Quantity
A small network with fewer, but stronger, connections will be much more effective than knowing hundreds of people but not having any depth to the relationships. If you have been a designer for a while chances, are you already have a number of contacts in the industry or in related industries. You may not need to meet a ton of new people in order to strengthen your network, you just need to get to know the people in your existing network better.

Particularly when it comes to social networking we tend to be consumed by numbers. Twitter followers is one example. But someone with 100 followers can have a bigger impact than someone with 1,000 followers, it's all a matter of the quality of the relationships. So do not be concerned with getting to know everyone out there, just focus on developing some quality connections.

It is not important that you have thousands of people in your network. What is much more important is the quality of those connections. The quality of your connections will involve how well you know the people in your network, how relevant your work is to one another, and the level of influence of each of you.

Whether intentional or not, most of us have an "inner circle" of people that are closest to us. This applies in social scenarios, such as students in a school, as well as in professional scenarios.

The goal is to have a few strong connections with successful people that will form your inner circle. These are the people that you will be able to reach out to when you need advice, to get answers to questions from their experience, and for help when you need it. And of course, they will be able to count on you for these things as well.

Do not dedicate all of your time to making new connections. Focus also on strengthening your existing connections and finding out which ones have potential to be a part of your inner circle.

7. People Do Business With People That They Like

While this may not always be the case, in general it is human nature to want to do business with people that we like. This concept applies to professional relationships. There are a lot of Professionals out there who can get the job done, depending on your needs. People in your network will want to work with someone that they like, not just someone who is good at what they do. Be yourself, be considerate of others, and be pleasant to work with. It will go a long way.

Looking at the same principle from another angle, it is not always necessary to have a specific purpose for networking with someone. You may get to know someone and enjoy connecting with them, but there is really no tangible benefit to either of you. That does not mean that there is no reason to continue to network with that person. Aside from your friendship, at some point in the future a situation might arise where there is a possibility to work together, and at this point if you already know and like each other you are that much closer to a win/win situation.

8. Be Proactive
If you are starting from scratch, you will need to take action in order to build your network. Once you reach a high profile in your industry or niche you will have plenty of people coming to you, but if you are just getting started you will need to be proactive in order to build your network.

Do not be afraid to reach out to people through contact forms on their website/blog, by email, or through social networks. It's a good idea to start off by interacting with them in the comments section of their blog and sharing their content via social media. This can help you to get noticed by others so that when you do reach out to them, they will be familiar with you, at least to some extent.

Many of the strongest connections I have made with other bloggers over the years started with me simply reaching out through a contact form on their blog to introduce myself and to compliment them on the blog.

9. Take A Long-Term Approach
Building a strong network, just like building a successful business, takes time. Of course, it is great when you can see the results of your networking efforts quickly, but the real value of those efforts will be seen in time.

Do not start your networking efforts with short-terms goals. Many bloggers consider networking to mostly consist of reaching out to other bloggers to ask for social media shares and votes to get more traffic for their latest post.

There is nothing wrong with asking your friends and contacts to consider sharing your content in the right situation, but networking should be much more than that.

Instead, work on building strong connections with no short-term goal in mind. If you are able to build strong connections with other bloggers in your industry or niche it will pay off in some way down the road. By focusing on a short-term goal you can damage your chances of establishing a true and strong connection with that person for the long term.

10. Do Not Focus Only On Industry Leaders
One of the mistakes that many persons make, in my opinion, when it comes to networking is that they focus exclusively on highly influential people. Sure, it would be great to get to know A-list professionals, but they have so many people contacting them on a daily basis that it is really difficult to make a true connection with them.

My preferred approach is to start smaller and connect with others who are at a similar stage in their career as you. This way you will both be able to help each other as your network grows, and it is far easier to develop connections with people who are still in the stage of working to grow their career. Most persons who are trying to grow in their careers are very open to connecting with other professionals and business owners, so it is generally pretty easy to develop some good connections.

You do not need to completely forget about networking with industry leaders but make that a much smaller part of your networking efforts at first. As your network, your career, and your profile within the industry grow, you will have better opportunities to connect with the most influential people.

11. Be Approachable
While it is important that you take action when it comes to networking, it's also important that others are able to easily reach out to you. Your website or blog should include a contact form that is easy to find, or at least list an email address where you can be reached.

In today's world of social networking, it's also a good idea to link to your profiles at sites like LinkedIn, Twitter and Facebook (or whatever social networks are popular with your audience) so others can reach you that way if they prefer.

Another part of being approachable involves responding to inquiries. Do you reply to comments left at your blog, to messages via social media, and to genuine inquiries through your contact form? If you respond to these types of inquiries it helps to show that you value the connections with your readers and followers, and it encourages people to get involved.

12. Set Aside Time For Networking
There are so many aspects to running a blog or a website and so many things that need to be done. It is very easy to overlook networking or to let other duties and responsibilities take a priority. But in order to build a strong network you will need to dedicate time for networking and connecting with others.

The best way to be sure that networking will not be overshadowed by other tasks is to set aside time in your schedule specifically for networking. It doesn't need to be a lot of time, but it should be a part of your daily, or at least weekly, schedule.

13. Be Organized
As your network grows it becomes increasingly important that you maintain some organization. You will of course, want to have easy access to the contact information of everyone in your network, and I also find it helpful to have a list of people that you consider to be in your network.

This list can be helpful for identifying people that you have not communicated with for a while, so you can reach out to them every now and then.

It is also helpful for seeing how your network grows over time as you add new people. If you categorize the list, you can even use it to help you identify the people in your network that you want to get to know better and, of course, when it comes time to ask for help from people in your network it is nice to have a convenient list.

A Good Network should be well organized. Well-structured from start to finish, that is what brings efficiency, effectiveness and excellence. A good network cannot survive without it.

Getting organized comes as second nature to some of us, while others may choose to procrastinate on any organizational tasks. For those people, just the mere thought of getting organized and putting things in order can be daunting.

Whether or not keeping organized is one of your strengths, it is a habit everyone should get into. If you have ever kept your boss waiting because you could not locate an important document, or if you are guilty of arriving late to meetings frequently or missing an important deadline, getting organized should be at the top of your to-do list.

It helps to improve your productivity in networking, by keeping organized, you will save time looking for things and will have more time to work on important tasks. As organization can improve the flow of communication between you and your team, you can also make your team more productive. After all, better communication leads to better results.

To be organized helps you to punctual consistently. Organization and punctuality go hand-in-hand. Consider setting calendar alerts, for example, to ensure you do not get too caught up in a task and lose track of time. Impress your manager, be prompt and show up on time.

You can ensure you meet deadlines. When task after task begins to pile up, it is not too hard to forget one small, yet important task. Do not miss an important deadline on a project because you got sidetracked with another urgent item. Set calendar alerts so you will never miss a deadline again. It enables you to complete your task ahead of schedule.

14. Network In Person, When Possible

There are so many great opportunities for networking online via platforms like LinkedIn that we tend to forget about all of the things you can do to make connections face-to-face.

It could take years of emails or messages through social media to reach the same type of connection that you could make with just a few hours of face-to-face contact. Whenever possible, make an effort to meet people in person. There are all kinds of conferences, seminars, and events in most industries that present extremely valuable networking opportunities.

Local organizations and chambers of commerce also offer plenty of networking opportunities. Social networks also make it possible to connect with others. If you are traveling you can easily post a message on Twitter about where you will be and when you will be there to see if people in that area would be interested in meeting up.

15. Hard Work

The most successful people make it look easy. But whether they are on a football field or in the boardroom, these well-known individuals did not make a name for themselves overnight. They put in many hours of hard work. Typically, someone will have tens of thousands of hours of hard work behind them before they finally achieve their dreams.

To get the desired outcome you have to put in the work. There is no by-pass for hard work, you ought to pass through the process efficiently and effectively to get the desired result. This takes diligence, devotion, determination, and discipline to achieve this.

Hard work applies everywhere it is not different with networking. Everyone involved need to put in the work to get the required output. It is the work you put in your network, that is the result you see.

Thomas Jefferson, former President and one of the founding fathers once said:

'I'm a great believer in luck, and I find out that the harder I work the more I have of it."

So, the more you put in the work in what you believe in the more opportunities that comes your way. What people call luck is when opportunity meets with preparation and it takes hard work to get there.

You may not be the richest one in the room; you may not be the smartest one in the room, but you have the duty to work the hardest to achieve your goals. It requires a lot of skill, time, resources to achieve a good network and hard work binds all these together. When everyone in your network plays their roles effectively your network will have greater significance.

16. Focus
When you are focused on what is important as regards networking, you tend to achieve so much and get above distractions. It is easy for you to give priority to what is important when you are focused and then you can achieve the desired result which is excellence in networking.

It also helps you in building relationships, as the goal is set been focused makes them achievable. Nothing is more powerful than focusing on the future dream and tasks the needed to be done now. Having the success roadmap, a strategically designed daily plan of action and the 'Just do it' attitude will eventually allow new habits to be formed. What was initially requiring great discipline is getting easier and easier as new habits are formed.

It is important that you stay extremely focused at the beginning so that you can create your own success fast. Small successes is a confidence booster! Your sponsor need not persuade you that this business works when you can enroll at least 1-2 people within the first month of joining the business. In Network Marketing, success is easier if we started on fast track.

Stay away from people or activities that can drain your energy. For example, recognize those dream stealers are avoid discussing your dreams with them. Negative news is another energy drainer for me to avoid. Maybe you would like to get rid of those in your life too.

Put in conscious effort to connect and associate with people who are supportive. It is very important to be with people who have a genuine desire to help us succeed. In Network Marketing, this is typically our mentor. For a stay-at-home mum, your spouse can be your prosperity partner if he too can see the brilliance of the Network Marketing business model. The Network Marketing Company's own corporate events are great ways to stay charged.

Focus requires a decision to be committed to seeing something through and when this is achieved the result is seen in your network. Focus needs consistency on your part and you can clearly differentiate from distractions.

You have to focus on the big picture, put your prospects or customers ahead of any quota you are trying to achieve. When you do this, you are truly focusing on helping the prospect. In the long run you will have better customers and better distributors.

Give each prospect his or her own index card or sheet in your notebook. That way your mind will not drift to the next phone call on your list.

You cannot eat with two forks at a time; devote your attention to one task at a time. You will accomplish more in the end. Think about it like working on a complex math equation. If you try to solve the problem all at once, the answer comes out wrong. Same goes for a prospect. If you try to solve all their obstacles at once, you will get frustrated. They will get frustrated, and you will get nowhere fast.

Your focus is elevated when you break down your goals. You can document your progress when you take each goal a step at a time. When you are breaking down goals, be sure to break them into actionable items you can track.

One day at a time approach works greatly to make you focus in your Network Marketing. At times it is a wild roller coaster. Every new distributor goes through it. You will too. Every millionaire in network marketing went through it. You will too, this is the number one reason why new distributors leave Network Marketing. Just about all new distributors go through this challenge. We call it the "Network Marketing Emotional Roller Coaster" and it can be an interesting ride during the frustrating times in this profession. So take this business one day, one call, one email, one moment at a time.

"Do not look for ways to save money, look for ways to make more money."

Travis Sims

CHAPTER TEN

SALES

We all need to be doing sales, some of us have difficulty in doing sales, while some people do not know how to approach it, and others do it wrongly. In this chapter, we will learn the most efficient way of doing sales.

The Seven Step Sales Process

1. Prospecting / Initial Contact
There are multiple ways you can get a prospect and also make an initial contact. You could be meeting people in a Networking event, it could be a referral from one person to the next, so you will have to reach out to that prospect and make the initial contact.
Always remember that first impression is Paramount when it comes to sales. People are sizing you up:
 -How are you dressed?
 - Are you standing up straight?
 - Are making eye contact?
 -What are you doing?

It is important to dress appropriately, be orderly and make a good first impression.
Do not go for sales immediately, it is a mistake most salespeople usually make. They want to go into the sale when they have not had a chance to get to know the prospect. Learn to be a good listener.

2. Qualifying
When qualifying your prospects, the following questions come to mind:

- Is this person a good sales prospect for me?
- Can I have a good relationship with this prospect?
- Will they be a good referral partner for me?

Remember in all these you have to qualify them, because they may not need what you have to sell. If you are trying to sell to someone, and they are not in the market for your product or services, they may even have no ability to use them, in such case you are simply barking up the wrong tree. You are using all this time and effort to push people away from you that could potentially be a good relationship and good referral partner for you.

You must qualify your prospects if they are good for you. Do they meet your list of qualifications to be a good prospect? If you do not have that list of qualifications, it is high time you make that list. What does your ideal customer look like? They must meet your qualifications to know that they are good prospect for you and if they are not your ideal customer, do not push it down their necks.

3. Needs Assessment

At this stage you are in this question process, you are talking, meeting, and getting to know them. You have to know what their needs are and assess the situation. Take time to build a relationship with your prospect, ask what their biggest successes are and what their biggest challenges are as a businessperson. Do a lot of listening and ask leading questions that feed into a potential sales opportunity for you. Make mental notes of how you can become a solution to the problems they are facing in business. You will tailor your sales pitch or demo focusing on fixing their problems with you as the solution.

4. Sales Pitch/ Product Demo
Now that you have listened and you have qualified your prospect, they show what their needs are, and you are able to meet them. You present the facts that you can solve their problems by giving your sales pitch or doing your demo. It is very important that you do it softly. You should not go for the hard sales or trying to cram it down their throats. You have to approach them in a soft way.

You are always going to stand a greater chance of winning over a prospect with a soft approach, even though they are not going to be do business with you for whatever reason it may be. It could be the price, but they will still be a good relationship and a good referral partner for you because of how you handled them. But when you hard sell and get "NO" repeatedly they are likely not going to have a good relationship with you and they will never refer you to others.

5. Proposal / Handling Objections
After you have given your sales pitch and demo, the next thing on board is presenting your proposal. Provide solutions to their problems, step back, and listen. When you offer the sale, you stop there. There is this silence, is this uncomfortable silence that most people want to pounce on but I encourage you to hold back when the awkward silence takes place. Let them talk, digest, and share with you what their objections are so that you can handle them in a really great and easy demeanor. In doing this, you will be able to help them walk through the objections as opposed to jumping in and jumping out without them having the time to digest it.

Now that you decided that this is a good prospect, they like what you have to offer, they are ready to buy from you because you are solving their problems and helping them to do it the right way. After achieving this, the next thing to do is to close the deal.

6. Closing

You should always use a contract when closing a deal, contracts are very vital for sales. Miscommunication tends to always give problems when closing a deal. So, it is important you are able to communicate effectively.

When closing a deal, I encourage you to have some type of template you can use to put in their names and figures. That takes away every form of guess work and misunderstanding. If you ever have an issue with the customers agreement or your fulfillment of the work, you can revisit the contract for clarity. Having a contract in place will also help you and your business look more professional in your sales process. A contract in place with the customer gives them confidence in their decision to use you and the trust that you will complete the assignment to the standards you both have set together. This allows the client to participate in the decision making during the closing.

7. Follow up/ Repeat Business/ Referrals.

It is great for you to follow up after closing a deal. Be appreciative, have an attitude of gratitude, send a thank you card, these all show your appreciation.

Ask for an opportunity to do repeat business with your client what else do they need done that you can help with? After all this person is pleased with the business you just completed with them, now is the best time to ask for future projects and seek referrals from them. It is also important to get introduced by those referring you. Your best opportunity to get a referral introduction comes immediately following the close of business when they are most satisfied. They are happy and excited and want to help you have success because of this. Asking for a referral now is the most opportune time.

Most Salespeople miss the aspect of follow up, repeat business, and referrals. They tend to neglect the fact that by doing all these it can result in more business to be done, and more referrals for the future.

Sales In Networking
Networking helps to make your sales rise, because when you network it is always an opportunity to meet more prospects and this can make your sales increase. You cannot ignore networking if you want to increase sales.

Networking is always going to provide the newest clients, best customers, and opportunities for you to do more business. It is a must for you to do networking and it can be done online. People are online now more than ever, so we all have to be doing more networking online. You need to leverage your social media and online presence for the sake of your business, because it can increase your sales.

"It is not about having the right opportunities; it is about handling the opportunities right."
Mark Hunter.

Tips From The AGC Process Of Networking
Accelerated Global Connections (AGC) was founded by me and I am the CEO of the Network. AGC started in the twin cities. We have over five hundred members now in six states and we are starting to scale out across the country.

The first thing to do is to connect to AGC events and get involved. Members likes to do business with other members and this principle does not only work with AGC, but it also works in any good networking group across the globe. This occurs due to the level of relationship and trust that has been built over time and clients will be more comfortable doing business with the people that they know because they all belong to the same organization.

In AGC it works by:

- Creating Opportunities
- Building Trust
- Get Connections
- Get Referrals
- Make sales

When all these happens, it can help to result in friendships and a long-term partnership in business, making sales and getting referrals.

How To Develop Your Sales Team

If you are an Entrepreneur or a small businessperson, and a team of one, you will have to rely on networking. It is important for your business to make sales as an Entrepreneur. As a Business Owner, you do not have the capacity or the budget to hire a Sales team or maybe you do not have the time to create a Sales team. By building and connecting in your network you can create a Sales team.

When you build relationships and people understand that you are good at what you do, they are most likely going to refer you. When you have built trust with them, they can easily refer you, and in that way, you have built a Sales team. This enables you to grow your Sales team exponentially.

When you have people talking about your products and your services, you also have people talking about how great they are, you are therefore expanding on your Sales team. People speaking on your behalf are giving you that word of mouth influence, they are helping you to get customers, they can become your Sales team and the beautiful thing about this team is that they are not on your payroll.

It is great if you appreciate them by sending them thank you cards and thank you gifts, but they are not on your regular payroll, these are just people inspired to help you, because they network with you.

I want to encourage you to stay and continue to do networking. It is not just about how you make sales; it is also very important to note how you develop your Sales team.

"The highest compliment you can give a business owner or salesperson is an introduction to your network."

Travis Sims

CHAPTER ELEVEN

THE BENEFITS OF BUSINESS NETWORKING

Business Networking is a really valuable way to expand your knowledge, learn from the success of others, attain new clients and tell others about your business.
These are the top 9 benefits for business owners of getting involved in networking:

1. Improve Your Profile
Being visible and getting noticed is a big benefit of networking. Make sure you regularly attend business and social events that will help to get your face known. You can then help to build your reputation as a knowledgeable, reliable and supportive person by offering useful information or tips to people who need it. You are also more likely to get more leads and referrals as you will be the one that pops into their head when they need what you offer.

2. Satisfaction From Helping Others
I really love helping other people, and networking is a fantastic way that allows me to do this easily. Networking is full of business owners that have problems or issues within their business that need solving, and there is great satisfaction from helping someone to solve a problem they have and get a fantastic result from it.

3. Friendship
Lastly, this one is more personal related rather than business related but is a big benefit none-the-less. Many friendships form as a result of networking because (mostly) you are all like-minded business owners that want to grow your businesses, and

you meet and help each other regularly, so naturally strong friendships tend to form. Some of my strongest friendships have been started from networking.

4. Opportunities
With a motivated group of business owners comes an abundance of opportunities! There are always lots of opportunities that come from networking and in fact this is where the benefits of business networking are huge!

Opportunities like joint ventures, client leads, partnerships, speaking and writing opportunities, business, or asset sales... the list goes on, and the opportunities within networking are really endless.

Just make sure you are jumping on board with the right opportunities and do not go jumping into every opportunity that comes your way. The opportunities that you get involved in should align with your business goals/vision, otherwise you might find that you are spinning your wheels chasing after opportunity after opportunity and getting nowhere.

5. Connections
"It is not WHAT you know, but WHO you know and how much you are known". This is so true in business. If you want a successful business, then you need to have a great source of relevant connections in your network that you can call on when you need them.

Networking provides you with a great source of connections, and really opens the door to talk to highly influential people that you wouldn't otherwise be able to easily talk to or find.

It is not just about who you are networking with directly either, that person will already have a network you can tap into as well.

So ask the right questions to find out if the person you are networking with knows who you want to know!

6. High Quality Advice
Having like-minded business owners to talk to also gives you the opportunity to get advice from them on all sorts of things related to your business or even your personal life and obtaining that important work-life balance. Networking is a great way to tap into advice and expertise that you would not otherwise be able to get hold of. Just make sure you are getting solid advice from the right person - someone that actually knows about what you need to know and is not just giving you their opinion on something that they have no or very little experience in.

7. Generation Of Referrals
This is probably the most obvious benefit and the reason most business owners decide to participate in networking activities and join networking groups.

The great news is that the referrals that you get through networking are normally high quality and most of the time are even pre-qualified for you. You can then follow up on these referrals/leads and turn them into clients. So, you are getting much higher quality leads from networking than other forms of marketing.

The increase in business from networking is the major advantage, but there are many others as well.

8. Increased Confidence
By regularly networking and pushing yourself to talk to people you do not know, you will get increased confidence the more you do this. This is really important as a business owner, because your business growth is very dependent on talking to people and making connections.

Networking is great for people that are not confident as it really pushes them to grow and learn how to make conversations and lasting connections with people they do not know. I was certainly not confident when I started networking, in fact it completely sacred

me! But as I do it more, the more confident I get and the easier it becomes, and the more benefit I get from it.

9. Positive Influence
The people that you hang around with and talk to do influence who you are and what you do, so it is important to be surrounding yourself with positive, uplifting people that help you to grow and thrive as a business owner. Networking is great for this, as business owners that are using networking are usually people that are really going for it, positive and uplifting.

SECTION THREE

THE MAGIC BEHIND NETWORKING

"Consistent actions brings about consistent results."

Travis Sims

CHAPTER TWELVE

THE MAGIC OF CONSISTENCY IN NETWORKING.

Consistency is the ability to replicate a process or activity with the same level of quality repeatedly. Trust is built in consistency because over time you are know for a particular thing, it becomes a brand, not having this face today and months later another face. People can only trust what the consistent and this is what brings confidence and trust while networking.

Dwayne Johnson a popular Hollywood Actor and Professional Wrestler quoted this saying:

"Success is not always about greatness, it is about consistency. Consistent hard work leads to success, greatness will come."

You can see this quote across board in business, entertainment industry, sports, politics and lots more. For example, Superstars like Roger Federer, Raphael Nadal and Novak Djokovic are known for professional tennis, they are consistent and excel over there. In Soccer you have Lionel Messi and Cristiano Ronaldo they have become household names for the sport the play. Basketball we have currently Lebron James, Steph Curry and lots more. People like consistency, they want to always see what you are famous for. They are all respected and regarded because of their greatness, but consistency brought them to that level of significance. It is quite easy to start and get to the top but when you get there that us where the work starts. These folks were consistent on what they do for a long period of time. This is also required for networking. When the network is formed, consistency plays a major role here the great amount of work to be placed here requires consistency.

Consistency requires staying true for what you stand for, for a long period of time and the benefits are massive to helping your network expand greatly. In consistency there is a lot of commitment, reliability, integrity placed into it to make it efficient, effective and excellent.

It is the key to networking, now just in networking but in everything. It plays a major role in networking, because it makes everything a great deal of improvement in it. You do not need perfection in your network, what you need is consistency. Success does not come from what you do occasionally, it comes from what you do consistently. Passion with consistency will always result to success.

Consistency is the best usability principle, when you are consistent Clients do not have to worry about what will happen. It brings about excellence in what you do, because indeed practice makes perfect.
You as a networker must have the attitude of not giving up, sticking to what works which is very important in networking. You automatically become a brand when you stay true. When you stay true it becomes your identity, networking business becomes a piece of cake.

The Greater Philosopher once said "We are what we repeatedly do"

THE RELEVANCE OF CONSISTENCY IN NETWORKING
Consistent actions bring about consistent results. So in networking you have to be consistent with your plans and whatever is brought to the table. The actions you take consistently brings out the result you want to see, consistently.

This principle in networking is brings about problem prevention rather that problem solving. When things are done right in a

consistent manner you will keep on preventing a problem, which is more effective.
But without consistency and allowing your results to develop, grow and prosper over time, you will not be able to get the success you are aiming for.

You will have to stay on course, if you want to grow an audience; you need to have a clear focus for your blog topics. While a range in your topics provides variety and may keep the attention of your audience, a very broad scope or even no topic focus at all will make it much harder for you to grow your audience.

Your niche does not need to be very narrow – but writing for young mothers one day and blogging about the best travel tips for bachelors the next will not only confuse what kind of audience you have. If your topics are not consistent, you may attract some chance readers for each of your posts. But you will not grow a returning audience
By been consistent you inspire trust with your audience, you build a relationship with your network grow your email list and customers. As trust come into play your network can only get better.

You do not give up too early, you may panic but you may know is part of the networking journey and without consistency and allowing your results to develop, grow and prosper over time, you will not be able to get the success you are aiming for. Panic leads to panic reactions and often those are fatal for networking success, because everything in networking needs time to grow and prosper. Panic is usually unnecessary and meager results are just part of starting out. There is so much you have to create, build and grow before that promised big-time success and it all has to do with consistency.

You also have to create content. It takes time to create so many posts that you can harvest the full power of social media and search engine for your traffic generation. Be consistent with your content creation. Publish regularly and grow your content hub.

An audience needs to grow. Never ever will you start something new and be famous with a huge audience after a couple of days. In the beginning, you will have a hard time to even make a handful of people aware of your efforts. But consistently providing value on your network and social channels will help you to attract, keep and grow an audience, brand and trust have to grow over time. If you meet new people, will you trust them as much as you trust your oldest friends? If you see a new brand coming up, how do you react to them? Most of the time it is a mild interest but still a little cautious. If you have the choice between the content of an established brand and a new brand you have never heard of, most likely you will choose the established brand. And consistency will help to grow your brand reputation.

You have to show one face to your audience, think about what face you want your audience to see from you - and then stick to it. If you are a young, boisterous, daring networker one day and try to come across as the serious and overly polite businessperson the next day, you can easily hurt your networking success. The reason is because; the two attract two different groups of people - even if you are still blogging for the same niche. Changing the face that you show to the public and your audience too much can confuse your audience - and prevent you from inspiring the trust you are aiming for. An inconsistent personality may just come across as dishonest.

We have worked with young entrepreneurs all looking for the one lucky punch. That might happen - for the lucky few. The broad mass of entrepreneurs has to work for success and growth, and that growth takes time to build up and prosper. Changing your strategy in quick succession is not the best way to build that growth. Not having a strategy at all and hopping from one idea to the next without any consistency is even worse for growth.

For Commitment one step is done before the other If you are starting out or your network and audience are still fairly small, you cannot act as if you are already running a famous blog with thousands of subscribers and followers.

When you are new to the networking consistency will also help you to stay focused and keep going. You have to work on the steps of your networking journey that are relevant now according to your networking experience and the state your network is in, and that is again where consistency needs to come into the game.

Do not get impatient and try to skip some important steps. There are steps you have to take first and others that only make sense if you do them after you did some of the others first.

Consistency is also the key to social media marketing success. Growing a social media audience takes time. You won't be able to start posting on social media and have a huge audience the next day. The path to social media marketing success lies in consistency: Figure out what your target group likes to get from you. Do more of that and see your audience grow.

Changing your activity and strategy all the time can well prevent you from growing an audience and seeing any kind of traffic success.

"Trust is what you need to get to in order to do more business."

Travis Sims

CHAPTER THIRTEEN
BUILDING TRUST

Trust is very important in your business, without it you cannot build better relationships with people, they cannot share their business with you, and will not pass you referrals without it. Trust involves integrity, sincerity, honesty, reliability, commitment, consistency, and competence. Trust is what we need to get to, in order to do more business.

"I learned to go into business, only with the people whom I like, trust and admire."
Warren Buffet.

What Is Needed In Building Trust

1. Be True To Your Word
If the desire is to be trustworthy, you must follow through with your word. You need to be the kind of person that does what they say you are going to do. You follow through and follow up, you are a person of word and action. People can trust what you are saying to them, when you say you want to do anything you actually does it. The number one thing in my opinion is that you are reliable. People can recommend you that you are true to your word.

2. Communicate Effectively
Most of the time when there is a disagreement with people it is a matter of miscommunication, when one or both parties are not communicating effectively. Be clear with your communication especially when it is a business deal, it should be in writing. It is important that you get the communication of your business deal

in writing, so that you can always go back to it to validate and revalidate the statements made by both parties.

Communicating effectively helps to promote a great level of understanding. If it is just for communication make sure that both parties understand. Do well to ask:

- Do you have any questions?
- Do you understand?

Communicating effectively is very important in building trust.

3. Build Trust Gradually

In building trust, you grow it gradually, you do not rush the trust, you allow it to grow gradually. Trust is something that must be earned. Trust is not given away easily; trust takes time to earn. Build it gradually, carefully, and considerably, so that you are trusting slowly, and people will trust you slowly as well. This concept is very important in sales, business, and in referral relationships.

People will not refer you except they know, like, and trust you. Trust is key in building relationships and trust takes time; it is important you build it gradually.

4. Make Decisions Carefully

When you are making your decisions, make sure you do so carefully. Think deeply about the decisions that you make. Make sure you are doing what you said you were going to do, because when you make a commitment and there is trust involved, people are going to expect that you follow through with your commitment.

Do not rush your commitment because it involves trust. When you make a commitment, you follow through with your actions. Do not rush to make the decision too early or too fast because you may find yourself back peddling to get yourself out from under those decisions and therefore it hurts your trust and your reputation. You will not be taken seriously because you do not follow through with what you said you were going to do. Make your decisions carefully and make sure they are made considerably.

5. Be Consistent
Consistency is key in building trust. For example, if I give you a job and you delivered excellently well. But at the second attempt in doing business with you there are disappointments and dissatisfaction. I will not refer you because you will not represent me well, but when you are consistent in doing business and your job execution is excellent, I will love to refer you to my other partners in business.

You will earn my trust when you are doing what you have agreed to do. Not only that, but you are doing it consistently. The more consistent you are in your delivery of top notch results the higher your level of trust from clients and customers will be.

6. Be Honest
It is important to be honest because your honesty brings about trust. You have to be honest no matter what, especially when dealing with customers, clients, and referral partners. People will respect you when you are honest with them. Even your Employers if you are not the owner of the business will honor you for that. It may be difficult sometimes to be completely honest, but as much as it concerns you be honest; it pays a lot to be honest.

Your level of trust will increase when you are honest. No matter how difficult it is people will always come back to you because of your honesty. People value people that are honest.

7. Participate Openly
Do not over promise. When you make a promise make sure you do your best to fulfill that promise. It is wise to promise what you

are able to do, and do not go above and beyond your means when you know fully well that you cannot be successful delivering it. When you make a promise make sure you are able to deliver at your word. If you have something that may come up and affect the job it is better, you bring it forward while negotiating the deal. We have all heard the saying "Under promise, over deliver." There should be an open communication between customers, clients, referral partners, and so on.

8. Help People

Look for additional ways to help the people that you do business with. Reach out to people possibly your clients, network, and ask how you can be of help to them. People will remember you for the right reasons that you offered to help them when they needed it the most and this action can help to build trust. You now become the person they know; they can call and count on.

You should learn to make it a habit of helping people consistently. When you are always helping others and giving it makes your trust level to go through the roof. When you help people get what they want, they will be willing to help you with what you want as well.

9. Show Your Feelings

The ability to show your feelings helps to bring out your sincerity. People want to know that you are real towards them, they want to understand that you are not a robot, they want you to actually feel for the people and know that you really want to help.

There is an old saying,
"People don't care how much you know, until they know how much you care."

This is very much a true statement. Work to make a personal connection with the people you do business with and it will make a huge difference in the bottom line of your business.

When you are authentic and you do business with integrity, people will want to tell others about you. Be a real person to the people you are trying to build a relationship with, and you will begin to get real business.

10. Avoid Self Promotion
This may be difficult for people because most people in business are always in sales mode.

The following questions always pop up in their heads like:

- How can I get the next sale?
- How can I get the next deal?

Even if they come up in your mind, you must do everything possible to avoid self-promotion, it is so much better for you to build relationships, develop trust then self-promotion may come up later. Trust will never come from self-promotion. It is ok to ask for referrals from those that you trust and from those that trust you, but you must avoid doing self-promotion all the time, because people will see you as an opportunist. They merge your trust to an ulterior motive in making sales; they will feel like all you have been doing is trying to get into their pockets.

If you are the type that always asks and never gives back, then you are gradually becoming less trustworthy. People will begin to avoid you because you are always promoting yourself.

Stop selling and start listening, and people will eventually ask you how you might be able to help.

11. Admit Mistakes
We are humans and humans make mistakes, not some humans but all humans make mistakes. If you think you do not make mistakes, you are mistaken because we all make mistakes. The key to trust is admitting that you are wrong.

Owning a mistake, being accountable and responsible for them is an important way for you to build trust.

You must seek for the following:

- How can I rectify this mistake?
- How can I overcome the mistake that I made?
- How can I sort this out, so it never happens again?
- How can I make this right?

When you make mistakes, you must learn to go over and beyond expectations, also do your best to over deliver. You over deliver in the next thing, so that people can clearly see and understand that this must have been a rare mistake, that you are not associated with failure, and disappointing your clients. They will be able to relate that the mistake is a rare one. You do your best to rectify the situation with them by taking note of the following:

- I must always admit my mistakes.
- I must make sure that I make it up to them.

In doing these, you can keep the trust you already have or re-earn the trust.

Trust takes a long time to build and a short time to discard it. We must trust slowly and discard fast. When you make a mistake; admit it, rectify it, and make sure you over deliver in recreating that trust.
People understand that mistakes happen its all how you handle the mistake that matters. If you admit the mistake, fix it promptly, and over deliver they will often become your best customer or referral partner because they will remember how you handled this sticky situation with honor and respect.

"Start the Culture, create the strategy and you will win."

Travis Sims

CHAPTER FOURTEEN
THE CULTURE OF NETWORKING

Just as networking is a way of life, culture is a way of life. Culture is important in business, teams, networks, groups etc. People actually think culture happens by accident, like there is no plan around culture, and this information is a misconception. It takes a conscious attempt to build a good culture. Some questions that may come to mind, for example:

- Where it comes from?
- How to find it?
- What it looks like?

Culture helps to create teamwork, success, growth, help etc. All these are correct, but it is also good to know about the structure of culture.

It is important when you create culture in your team, business, workplace, organization, there are some important questions that may arise.

- Are you on the right team?
- Where is the right team?
- Do you need to leave your present team?
- Do you want to leave the team because you are not part of the culture?
- Do you want to be on the team because you want to be a part of the culture?
- Do you just want to dive in and see how the culture works?

Define Your Culture
If you are a leader, business owner, the team captain, the head of your organization or business. It is up to you to define your culture. You have to steer the culture, and this does not happen by accident, it starts by leadership. Leadership helps to steer the culture, although it does not completely define the culture. The entire team is going to make it up. The Leader's job is to steer the team in the right direction.

Everyone Contributes
I do this a lot when forming teams, I ask the following questions:

- What is the most important thing to you as a Business owner, Entrepreneur, Salesperson, etc.? Sum it up in one word.
- What does the culture need to be?
-What are your core values?
-What does the quality need to be?
   The answers I mostly get regarding the above questions are:
-Relationships
-Trust
-Integrity
-Referrals
-Closing lots of businesses
-Accountability
-Best use of time etc.

One way to help start the culture and keep it in place is to share it regularly. Place your culture listed out on the wall, on your website, in your handbook. Keep it visible at all times so that every person on the team can see it easily and know it easily. Here is a way to state your culture:

- This is the culture that we are creating.
- This is the culture that we have.

They can be bought into, only when there is a good team atmosphere.

Team Atmosphere
It is great to create a team atmosphere; a single person cannot create the culture. It takes effort of a team to create the culture. In a team atmosphere, everyone is participating, engaging, and contributing to the success of the culture in the business. When creating the team atmosphere, you must know that it is important that you create the mission.

Mission
Everyone in the team must know what the mission is, and they can repeat it. So many times, some companies create a mission, and it is never revisited again. I always ask myself whenever I am creating something new:
- Does it support our mission?
- Does it help create our mission?
- Is it true to our mission?

Mission is an important aspect in creating culture.

Vision
Vision is the long-term thing; we do not need to know exactly how we are going to get there but you must know that it is about what we want to create, and this is the direction to achieve it. As a leader in the organization, creating the vision is a very important aspect of creating a culture.

One of the biggest visions in history was when US President John F. Kennedy shared "We are going to put a man on the moon, and we are going to do it in this century." There were parts of this vision they had no idea how they would accomplish it. They knew how to get people to the moon, but they did not know how to get them back safely and this was an important part of the equation. When creating a vision, you only need to know this is what we want, and this is the direction we are going. However, it is not enough to just have a vision; it is very important that you have goals along with it.

Goals

The vision is the long-term thing, but these are the goal posts to hit along the way when you are heading toward the vision. Just as vision is the long-term thing, goals are the short-term small steps to accomplishing your vision. It is what you plan to accomplish, you are going to create a plan around it and make sure it is achievable. It helps you in creating accountability around it so that you can hit the goals along the way to the vision. When creating goals make sure they are just out of reach but not so far out of reach, make sure they are realistic and accomplishable. Every goal post we hit, we strengthen the culture of the team, group, organization, company, etc.

Like Minded People

In creating your culture, you have to get people that are like minded. You also want people that have a common theme with you. They fit within your culture, and they align with your core values. People who are investing, engaging, agreeing to participate. It is great to have like-minded people, but you also need some diversity in creating your culture.

Diversity

Diversity is very important in creating the best in your culture. Not only people that are like minded with a common theme but also those that think, and act differently could be very helpful in creating culture.

In diversity, it cuts across different race, sex, culture, and religion etc. So that you can get views for unity from different places and walks of life. Your culture needs to appeal to a wide range of people, in culture there is unity in diversity.

Safe Space

In creating culture, a safe space is an important place to be. I can be sharing my views and I do not have to be worried that I will be called under the carpet later. It is a safe place to be because people can be comfortable with it, but when it is not a safe place; people will stay clear from it. People will be afraid of sharing their thoughts because they are afraid of being reprimanded or being made fun of because they shared their thoughts.

You often hear presenters say

"There is no such thing as a stupid question."

The reason they say that is so that people can be free to ask any question, it helps to create that safe place so that people can participate. This is very important while creating your culture.

I once had a person on a team I was managing that constantly challenged me. This person would consistently ask me why are we doing it this way. Have you considered it another way? Is this the best approach? Have you thought of all the causes and effects? They challenged me at my every move and others on the team would ask why do you keep this person on the team? I responded that I want someone who is challenging me and pushing me towards excellence. This is how we take a team and make it better, how we develop a team of excellence.

Strive For Excellence
You want people in your network to strive for excellence. Why settle for the mediocre when you can do so much more. In building a culture of people that strives for excellence, they have to be motivated and encouraged to up their game, keep it at a high standard within the culture. This is also why you hire up. When bringing someone onto the team try to hire or bring on people who are better than you. Work to bring on people who could replace you if need be. This determines the direction of the team. If you do the opposite and bring on only people who are less than you or yes people that never challenge you to think in new ways you will take the team in the wrong direction. Hiring up keeps the team growing towards excellence.

Reward and Recognition
When you are asking people within your network to strive for excellence, it is important you also place the importance of reward and recognition, because they strived for excellence. You reward and recognize those upping their game and taking the business or organization to the next level. Rewards for those hitting above the levels, for those going above and beyond. It is important you do not do this privately. You reward and recognize people publicly; it is important for steering people to strive for excellence. This helps to create an environment of positivity and this will encourage everyone to give their best. It helps to improve the morale and the energy of the team.

Hold Them Accountable
Accountability helps to create that productivity within the team or organization. Some managers tend to micromanage, they tend to hold everyone on the team accountable and they do things stereotypically, but there are also managers that allow some room

of freedom, they allow the people working with them the room to be creative, add their input and their style, at the end of the day the are still held accountable for the goal of the organization. Great accountability is welcomed by the team when it aligns within the culture and core values. Helping the team to stay above the minimum standard and striving for excellence. When using accountability it is important that everyone on the team understands what that standard is and what is the vision for the organization, all of this ties together to create the culture of your team or network.

Offer Some Grace
It is very important you offer grace because we are humans and human make mistakes. We as leaders also have to take ownership of the shortcoming. Did you communicate the goal and the mission clearly; did you do your part and offer support? For example, when someone falls short of the goal you can offer grace by saying:

 - Let us do better next time.
 - How can I better support you?
 - How can I lift you up?
 - How can I help you achieve the goal next time around?

Fire Fast
When someone you invited who now belong to the team, is just not merging with the culture of the team, they do not want to achieve the goal of the team, not interested in the vision and mission of the team, all they do is to add negativity and bring everyone down, this person must be removed from the team as soon as possible, so they do not damage the core of the team.

You must always consider this:

"Can one person build or create the Culture of the team?"
Always remember that a spark can create a huge flame either for positive or negative. I always say:

- Hire slow
- Interview well
- Fire fast especially if the person is not measuring up and they bring negativity within the group, so that they do not pollute the rest of the team.

Get Social
You have to keep the fun in the fundamentals. It cannot be all work and no play. I know for some of us that statement is very difficult to bring to reality especially when you are goal focused, you are the type that loves your job so much to the extent that it does not feel like a job to you. They have fun while working, but nevertheless I encourage you that as a leader trying to build a great culture in your team to put something in place that will get everyone social.
It could be a fun contest that causes creativity and productivity. It could be a contest that result to prizes for those who have done well, it could even be seeing a movie together outside work just to get everyone social and add some level of fun in the group. Some companies do outings as well, reward breakfast, in all these the goal is to get everyone on board to be social, it is part of the culture.

Take An Interest
We are all humans, we want to feel loved and liked by others, we want to fit in and participate. It is important for a leader trying to create a good culture in their team to take interest in the people

you are leading and working with, do well to also listen to them, people tend to appreciate those who give them a listening ear. Take interest in them, get to know:

 - How are they doing?
 - How are they working?
 - The Project they are currently working on?

It is great to take interest in people and see how you can be of help to them.

Promote Self Care
There is a reason why there is a 40-hour work a week not a 60 or 80 hour-work a week. I understand that entrepreneurs and solopreneurs may say that they do lots of 80-hour weeks, it is simply because they work for themselves. Even as important as your job is to you, it is advisable that you take some time off for yourself. As a leader who wants to create a great culture within your group, team or organization to also create that time for others in the team.

Your team will be more productive when they are well rested, happier in their workplace and they know that they have a Leader that cares about them and their wellbeing.

Emphasize Purpose
"Culture eats strategy for breakfast"
Peter Drucker

When emphasizing purpose these questions come to mind:
 - Are we on the right track?
 - Is our culture in place?

This is why when I am helping organizations to create a close network, I always keep communication at the front of them because I want the team to know that what they are doing matters. Understanding the purpose and making your team understand the purpose is very important.

Stay Focused
As a Leader of your team, you want to help your team to create this focused mentality. You want them to focus on the task and not get distracted. If you start up with lots of ideas, do well to implement them. This is when your dream comes true, but ideas without implementation is only a daydream, because at the end nothing will be done.

Be Transparent
As a team it is important to know that we are winning. Is important you let them know that we just accomplished this great feat, and they should also know when the team is losing. You can be transparent by stating that:

 - Here is why we are losing?
 - This is how we are losing?
 - What are the ideas that can help us bring a solution to the problem.

It is always important to recognize as a Leader trying to create a healthy culture in the team, that focus is not to only take the glory and when things go bad you do not share the pitfalls with others in the team. When you do this, it shows you are not transparent, and it is not good for leadership.

You always need to be transparent with your team, so that they can be part of the solution to the problem. Be transparent, allow members of your team or organization to know they have to work harder because the team is losing and not doing well at the moment. You can also encourage them when the team is winning, celebrate in the good times. In all of these it is great to be transparent; it helps to build a great culture within the team.

"Opportunity does not occur while sitting on the sidelines."

Travis Sims

CHAPTER FIFTEEN

THE POWER OF TEAMWORK IN NETWORKING

According to Andrew Carnegie, Teamwork is the ability to work together towards a common vision. The ability to direct Individual accomplishment towards organizational objectives. It is the fuel that allows common people to attain uncommon results.

Teamwork makes the dream work. Develop lots of great team of people around you. My favorite acronym for Team is

T- Together
E- Everyone
A- Achieves
M- More.

We surround ourselves with a team to help us get to the goals. If you help enough people to get what they want they will help you get what you want also.

A good team provides compelling directions and goals. Surround yourself with the like-minded people that have the same views as you and also the people that challenges you to become better, and to develop personally and professionally.

In a good team, they ought to share and have the same mindset. They have the same goals, they are contributing to the success of the network, they help one another, they have long term vision, mission, and goals. They are all in agreement.

A Great team has a strong structure. They meet regularly at the same place and time; they do everything together. They have an agenda that they are all meant to accomplish. They make good use of their time.

Time is our biggest asset; you can make more money, but you cannot make more time. We all have 24 hours in a day. No one has higher amount of time than the other. No one has 25 hours, and another get shortchanged with 23 hours. It does not happen that way we all have the same amount of time.

A good team is supportive, and everyone has a voice. When you involved in transactional business and involve in allow finances a good relationship is not formed but when you involve in relational business a better relationship is formed. With relational business, people tend to have a better relationship with you and will help you with referrals and recommendations when the need arise.

Find out how to be supportive, be encouraging with your voice and your actions, it makes a lot of impact in networking. Been supportive has a huge amount of value in teamwork.

It is always great to evaluate your team, especially your team members. Ask questions like:

Is this the right team for me?
Why am I in this team?
Is the team meeting my goals?
Am I with the right team members?

You will have to answer these questions. You get to decide, because you are the one in charge of your own destiny, so you get to decide. You must decide which team you want to participate in and make sure it is high functioning goals.

You team mates should be goal focused, they will help you network up!. Network with people that are smarter, richer, has better business, know more people than you. These are the persons you ought to spend your time with. You are a product of the five persons you regularly spend your time with. If you are the richest, smartest, biggest person in the room then you are in the wrong room. You have to network up by networking with the people better than you.

A good team makes high quality decision regularly. You can hold each other accountable to those decisions, you make those high-quality decision together.

There are 5 things that makes up a good Team:

-Good communication: You must make sure everyone in the team are connected together in communication. It brings forth your relationship and transparency. Everyone knows their decisive roles; they are accountable to one another.

-Delegation: You cannot do it all on your own. You need reliable hands that you can delegate duties to. For example, a person may be very good at social media and the arrangement regarding social media is delegated to the person. The same with structuring, communication etc, you delegate roles, each person work in their area of strength and this can make the team efficient.

-Efficiency: This is the good, important, effective, and productive use of time to grow exponentially, both personally and professionally. In our business we can accomplish so much in a day because we have an efficient team. It enables you to maximize time excellently and whoever is able to do that is successful.

-**Idea Bank:** A good team is a reservoir of ideas, these ideas is what makes the network productive. These ideas enable the team to achieve their goals. Team share ideas and they should be free to contribute with their ideas.

-**Supportive:** Even the most successful people in the world have bad days and no one is immune to it. You should have a team of people to lean on at difficult times. Supportive teams help to bring encouragement, ideas, content, and they bring their voice to the table. They will do all to achieve the common goal.

Teamwork is important to the success of any organization and the opportunity for individuals to work together towards achieving a common goal. The benefits of teamwork are huge, not only for the individual and the business, but also for the relations between other companies that work with yours.

"Referrals are the best way to say thank you for great service."

Travis Sims

CHAPTER SIXTEEN

REFERRALS

Referrals is done by directing someone you know to another who is great in that field for services, sales, advice and so on. Referrals is taking the time to introduce you to someone you do not know on your behalf.

The reason why people do not just give referrals, it is because it involves a high level of trust. It takes time to build trust. Overtime if you have been reliable, responsible and you are able to always deliver, the tendency will so high because of your track record. Trust is the biggest hurdle; it takes time to build trust.

In referrals you must know that it is the referrer's reputation that is on the line, so the person been referred have the obligation to perform excellently and efficiently.

It is the best type of advertisement you can possibly do. The word-of-mouth way is so effective. It is still a great form of advertisement even till today, it never gets old.

For example, you went to a restaurant in town. The management of the place met your expectations, good waiting, good meal, well ventilated and so on. At the end of the day, I may not refer that restaurant to my friends, family, and associates simply because it was just good. Nothing above the normal, nothing extra that every nice restaurant will not be able to render. But when the restaurant go above your expectations, they do the extra, It may be discounts, bonuses, more value, good follow up and feedback mechanism. Then with all these, you will be motivated to tell your friends, families, and associates about it free of charge. It does not cost money to simply refer.

HOW TO GET REFERRAL PARTNERS

1. Be Grateful
Learn to be grateful, have the attitude of gratitude. You have to say lots of thank you; it can go a long way of leading to the pot of gold. This is instrumental in networking.

2. Take Great Care of Your Client
After receiving that Client through referral from a friend or business associate the least you can do is to take great care of your client. Render great services above and beyond his or her expectation so that your client will always return and better still continue to preach the gospel about your business. Always remember that the reputation of the one who referred the client is at stake, so you will do well to give your best in an excellent and effective manner.

3. Reciprocate
Do not just be a receiver, also learn how to be giver. Networking excels with the abundance mindset, so is not just all about me, myself, and I, the foundation of networking is helping others, while doing that your needs are also met.
You must learn how to reciprocate effectively. Your Colleague or Associate should not be the only one bringing business and Clients, you also do likewise, so that the chain can continue and everyone is successful.

REFERRAL PROGRAM

The days of hanging a shingle and waiting for business to come are over. People were lucky with such mindset in time past, whereby they were only interested in transactional business but today that method no longer yields much. To have an excellent referral program it has to go beyond that transaction, it should be relational business, whereby you have a good relationship with your customers. You must pay good attention on how to get future deals.

When having a referral program, and you aim to have future deals, you must ask yourself the following questions:

- Am I training my Referrer Partners?
- Am I consistently meeting new people and opportunities?
- Am I investing into the program?
- Am I consistently meeting with people in my network?
- Am I just attending and not participating?
- Am I taking action?
- Do I have a good referral program?
- Do I have a team of people around me?

High level quality of follow-up and connection with the people in the network should be done to achieve excellence, effectiveness and efficiency in your business.

For example, in Accelerated Global Connections (AGC); you can connect with over Five hundred person, over 2000 persons to network with on Facebook. You have to use such opportunities to network, build relationships, develop trust, share business, and get referrals.

In achieving these you must engage deeper to achieve your goals, more actions and more work. The business you admire and will love yours to emulate they also took action and did the work, not is your turn, hit the thread mill.

THE IMPORTANCE OF REFERRAL NETWORK

1. You Will Be Part Of An Exclusive Community
The other members need you just as much as you need them, so the quality of experience and knowledge is crucial to all involved.

2. Advisement
Once you are involved in referral network, that feeling of "being alone" while running your business is gone. The other members of the group turn into business advisors of sorts and vice versa.

3. Collaboration Is The Name Of The Game
You may find someone in the group that is a perfect fit to work on a project with you. Or you may be the ideal person to help another member as well. The group works together collaboratively, to achieve more together.

4. Extend Your Network
Joining a referral network expands your network exponentially and rapidly. If you are in business, you know how important your network is. By joining, you instantly add to your network and typically gain the networks of those in the group with you. It's vital in any business or professional pursuit to establish connections in the community. These relationships can serve as information resources and business partnerships and as an avenue to influential individuals who may be able to provide you with advice and mentoring opportunities.

5. New Learning
Everyone in the network is unique in skill, experience, and connections. By interacting and sharing your challenges, it is almost sure that someone in your group will have a solution for

you and you may also be able to offer a solution, connection or tactic to help another in the group.

6. Cross-promotion

When you join a referral network, you will most likely find ways to help each other by utilizing cross-promotion. Finding ways to help each other through promoting to your respective networks. It is safe to assume that each person within your referral circle has his or her own network, and the services you offer as a health and fitness professional may be enticing to another individual within your contacts' networks. You refer clients to those in your network for services you cannot provide and, in turn, they send potential clients to you.

7. Think Bigger

Being in a network, you cannot help but think bigger and stretch beyond your boundaries when surrounded by amazing people doing amazing things.

Referral networks are incredible and can do wonders for your business. Growing in a group is not only more effective, but It is also quite a bit more fun!

By joining you will increase your exposure to like-minded professionals, gain referrals from a network and sharpen your networking skills. Develop lasting relationships that allow you to grow personally and professionally.

"If you are the best connected, richest, and most successful person in the room... You are in the wrong room."

Travis Sims

CHAPTER SEVENTEEN

NETWORKING UP

These questions will show if you are truly networking up:

-Are you in the right room?
-Are you with the right people?
-Are you improving your networking level?
-Are you still the same?
-Are you declining because of who you are networking with?

My Dad used to tell me all the time: "Son, you are known by who you run with." Dennis Sims

This was a nice way of telling me that I was making the wrong friends, that I needed to choose better friends. This was early advice for me as a teenager, which made me grow even professionally. Because of this great advice, I always check to see if I am networking with the right people.

Are you networking in the right room?
You should not get satisfied staying too long in your network especially when you are not growing. Are you improving and moving forward personally and professionally?

It comes with this old adage that says:
"Big fish in a small pond."

Are you the smartest person in the room? Then you are in the wrong room. If you are the biggest fish in the pond, I believe it is the right time to change your location so that you are not biggest fish anymore. With that you will be able to network with people that are more successful than you. You network with people that

make more money and are smarter than you. This approach will help you move up in your network and this is what we call networking up.
Your food of thought is this:
Are you networking up?

Important Points To Help You Network Up

1. Network With Successful People
To network with successful people, the set of questions that comes to your mind are:

-Where are successful people?
-Where are they hanging out?
-Where are they spending their time?
-Are you spending your time with them?

For you to network up in your career or your business, you need to locate successful people, find out where they meet, and where they spend their time.

During the recession of 2008, a Lexus dealership recognized that their clients were not coming in anymore and the sales floors were sitting empty. They decided to go where their clients hang out. They sent their salespeople out to country clubs, golf courses. They would make small talk with people networking and pretty soon someone would ask; "What do you do for a living?" The salesperson would say I am a Lexus salesperson have you ever driven one? Before long they were out on a drive in a brand-new Lexus enjoying all that comes with a new car. At this point the salesperson knows you don't want to go get back in your old car and offers to make them a good deal. You see, Lexus knew to survive the recession they needed to go network up where their clients were hanging out. Go network in country clubs, golf courses, cigar lounges, high quality networks like AGC, and private clubs. To truly network up you must go where successful people spend their time. Knowing all this helps you to play your role in locating them and spend time with them. In achieving this you will have to embrace discomfort by leaving your comfort zone, being authentic, you do not sell yourself, you stay positive, and you add value to the people around you.

2. Embrace Discomfort

To excel in your career or in your business, you must go outside of your comfort zone. It will make you uncomfortable to leave your comfort zone. If being successful is the goal, then it is inevitable. If you are comfortable in staying in your comfort zone you will reach a roadblock, and that will be your ceiling, you will not improve in your network. Leaving your comfort zone enables you to move forward in your career or business.

It is quite easy to stay in your comfort zone. You are always with the same people every week; you have the same conversations every time. You are not really growing, and your associates are not growing as well. They may see it that it does not really matter, they may feel it's just what they do and they are quite comfortable with it.

Life begins at the end of your comfort zone. A successful career originates when you embrace the discomfort that comes from going out of your comfort zone. It is not going to be easy because you are not used to it, but do not feel discouraged, do not be intimidated. You must not be intimidated by successful people or with people with a higher social-economic status. If you are intimated by them then you will not network up or even get to their level. You must go outside your comfort zone so that you can excel in whatever you do.

3. Be Authentic

When you go outside your comfort zone and meet successful people, the next thing to do is to be authentic to the people you meet. It is very simple to be yourself. Look great, get all you need to look great. It goes with the saying:
"You are addressed by the way you are dressed."
It is great that you get a nice outfit, it attracts people to you, but you retain the relationship by being authentic. It takes less effort on your path to simply be yourself. Do not be fake or try to imitate others.
People like you for who you are. Dress for success, but do not try to be someone else. People will like you because you are authentic, you are true to yourself. Be the best version of yourself. Think of it as you are on a first date. Be your most authentic self, it is very good for business. Dress for success but do not be someone else. People will enjoy knowing the real you.

4. Do Not Sell

I know we all are salespeople, and it comes naturally to us, especially when you remember that your goal is to meet with successful clients and to do everything possible to sell what you do and what you have to them.

In this situation you must be disciplined not to sell at the first opportunity. The urge will be there because you are fully aware that meeting with these successful people will make a huge difference in your career. You strongly believe that they can invest so much into your business, they can buy so much from you, but hold back and do not sell. They will seek you out and eventually ask you.

-What do you do?
-How long have you been doing this?
-What do you love about it?
-How are you different from others?
-How are you making a difference?

-What makes you unique and special?

All these things are going to pop up during your conversation when you decide to hold back, and you do not sell. Do not push it, just allow it flow naturally. With this move someone may be interested to take a chance with you. They may even be impressed by you and what you do and want to get involved as well. Hold back, do not sell, just let it drip in. Get more information, get to know them, build relationships, and build trust. Drip it in and they will be so impressed to the extent that they want to do business with you.

This is way better than selling to them and being opportunistic with your dealings with successful people, you will just look like the others. You will look unique and special when you act this way. It is a longer approach, but it is a more fruitful approach in achieving success. If you do this overtime, they are going to spend more money with you because you have earned a higher trust with them, there is commitment and loyalty on your path.

Successful people may even make referrals for you. They will network with their other successful friends and introduce you personally to them and that is good for business. You will get more referrals in the future because they have come to like your style and how you do business with people.

There are some benefits when you do not hard-sell;

-They spend more money
-Build better relationships
-Develop trust
-Get referrals

5. Stay Positive
You must always stay positive while networking with successful people. Successful people do not network with negative people,

so it is important to always remain positive no matter what. They do not do business with pessimist and downers.

Successful people do not have time for pessimism. They do not want to use their energy for negativity. When you are not positive, you do not belong there, they simply have nothing to do with you. People are naturally complainers, they tend to complain about everything, they complain about the Economy, the Stock Market, the Government, the weather, Coronavirus policies, and so on. But during all this, always try as much as possible to stay positive.

Always try to see the good in everything because people do not like bad news, they only want to hear good news and not bad news. So, you always have to stay positive. Successful people always love to be around people with a positive mindset, it is a great asset to them.

In life people need to be lifted up, build courage, build confidence, build positivity and if you do these things people will be naturally attracted to you. You will be like a magnet to successful people.

Do well to repel negativity, people going through difficult times need a lot of positivity and not negativity. People that are negative truly have nothing to offer, they are toxic to the environment, but the positive ones have a lot to offer.

Positive people attract like-minded people. Say positive things, share positive things, and stay positive. The people you are networking with will be more attracted to you because of your positivity.

6. Add Value
It is great to stay positive, but what keeps you longer and valuable to successful people is when you add value. Know your craft, never go out unprepared, know the current happenings, the current topics, and be vast in your Industry.

If you are going to a golf club, be ready to talk about golf. Always be ready to be in conversation, positive conservation and always add value to your audience.

People always remember you when they know that you always bring something to the table, meaning you always add value. You can add positivity to every place and everything and then you will become valuable to that network.

7. Follow Up

No matter how the conversation was, never assume that people are going to remember you. They have a lot that they are dealing with, follow up will need to address that part. Follow up is great, the fortune is always in the follow up. Follow up creates the building blocks for creating and developing a good relationship with people and building trust with your proposed clients. The role of follow up in networking is essential. When networking up these are the tools that enables you to reach higher levels of success, to also meet higher levels of people that can be instrumental to you achieving your goals. It is not enough to just be comfortable; it is not enough to just stay in your comfort zone and just stay in your network with little or no growth. If you desire to have a higher level of success, income, and relationships you must network up.

"If you are networking with only people who look like you, think like you, and do business like you, you need to diversify your network."

Travis Sims.

CHAPTER EIGHTEEN

DIVERSITY WITHIN YOUR NETWORK

You can ask people that are into business and career, how many networking groups they belong to, they may just say one networking group. You cannot be in one networking group with just twenty people that look like you and think like you that is located within 30 minutes of your house or work and say that you are networking. How many women are in your group of 20? How many African Americans, Latino businesses, LGTBQ, in what generations? What about the businesses from neighboring communities, around your city, in your state, nationally, and internationally?

The advice from me is that you need to expand your diversity within networking.

How Can You Grow By Using Your Network Exponentially?

1. Network With Women In Business
If you look at networking holistically you will be able to see that it is heavily dominated by men in business. Most networking groups have about 70-75% of men in business. Work force is a good contributing factor to this because more men are working and are into business compared to women. In the general population of the world, you have 50% of women. Now if you are not networking with women, you have missed a whole lot of opportunities.

It is a missed opportunity not to network with women because they represent some of the best minds in the world. There have been women leaders and great women in their profession and businesses for a long time. If you have been networking and you did not add women to the picture, you have been missing out. I encourage you today to make practical steps and actions in networking with women. It will help you network up in whatever you do. Women tend to be more relational rather than transactional when it comes to networking and business. This is really the best approach when it comes to networking and makes them very skilled in the relationship process. Be sure to connect with women business leaders authentically and remember networking events are not bars to pick up women. All women deserve a safe place to network their businesses.

In Politics, Businesses, Careers, Sports, and lots more, there are women championing the events as well as the men. In Networking with women, you will need a great part of their ideas and advice. For example, the products you want to send to the market;

- How do women see it?
- How do women view the messages that you are sharing?
- How do women view your marketing and advertising?

It is great to have women on the inside, they can help guide you through the ropes. If you are not networking with women, you are missing from the 50% of the population which could have helped to steer your business to a better position. It is very important to connect with women as a business owner.

2. African American Community

In this, we are not just talking about those in the United States only, but we are talking about people of color around the globe. You do not have to see them as a little group or a minority group in your community; you will be getting the wrong picture of things. If you are not networking with this community, you are missing out big time.

The African American community boasts of some of the best minds, some of the world changers, great professionals in sports, medicine, politics, law, etc. If you are not networking with the

African American community, it is time you start doing so because their impact to your business is massive. In this it can enable you to network up. Do well to connect with them on LinkedIn, Facebook, Twitter, Instagram, or any social platform you are engaging with today, it is important you connect with them.

Start building relationship with them, develop trust and start diversifying with this group of people that is the only way you can network up. This can help you in excelling in your business, content, and getting referrals etc. The opportunities that come from networking with them are great.

3. Support Latino Business

As a good networker you should not miss any section of the community. You do not become bias by supporting with a community above others. If you want to excel in your network, you must learn to be involved with every segment of the community. You must remember that every part of the community makes the whole, so they are all important. None of a community group should be sidelined or left behind.

There are important questions you must put in place.
- Are you engaged with those in business?
- Are you having conversations with their leaders?

If you exempt this group from your network, it will affect your network from improving. Aside from the network, let us say for your business and you want to make sales and you are missing this whole block of people, a whole block of population to the market to, to grow from, and those that can buy from you. So obviously you are missing out big time, you are been distracted and not focused. If you only want to do business with those that looks like you, that thinks like you, then you are missing out from what you could have used to your advantage for the advancement of your business.

Do well to support Latino business. Get connected with them because they have great amount of purchasing power. Make great effort to connect with Latino businesses.

4. LGBTQ Community
The LGBTQ community has their own chamber of commerce. Anyone that wants to excel in networking will learn not to segregate. For example, in the Twin Cities LGBTQ Community have a great voice. Doing business with them in such areas can be of immense opportunity for you.

Love all people, give everyone equal opportunity to do business with them. In this way you can diversify your network. Look for ways to get involved and support pride activities and meet LGBTQ businesses.

5. Generations
Generations play a vital role in diversification when you network with these groups.

The different generations include:
  A) Baby Boomer Generation (1946- 1964)
  B) Generation Jones (1955- 1965)

Are you networking with these generations?
People usually say it is more effective to network with the young, the recent, the millenniums, the tech people etc. But there is a lot to gain while networking with these generations.

They are often of the CEO level; they are already in high level management and they can provide relevant information and advice from their perspective. By disregarding them, you are missing out on a lot of things. You have a lot to learn from them.

These questions may arise while networking with these generations:

- How do your Seniors see my business?
- What is their perspective about your marketing and sales strategy?
- Are you seeing them as mentors?
-Can they potentially serve as mentors for you?

These generations in networking helps to provide you with great opportunities to gain knowledge, expertise and mentoring from them. They have been there before, they have done it before, they have gone through the thick and thin. They have been through the recessions; they may have even experienced a pandemic before. They are the type of people that you can gain that kind of experience from. This is a great opportunity to dig in from the successful people that have been there before us.

C) Generation X (1965- 1980)
These are the middle age group of people and they have some experience under their belt, they have been through a few things, they have hit that mid-level management or above it. You are greatly advised to reach out to such people because you can benefit immensely from their wealth of experience. I fall into this category of Generation X.

D) Xennials (1977- 1983)
They have their own share in the successes over the years and their wealth of experience can also be of help to the present-day business owners and professionals that are into networking.

E) Millennials (1981-1996)
They are also called Generation Y. Everyone is saying we should be doing more business with millennials. They are the decision makers; they are the up-and-coming business owners and entrepreneurs.

F) Generation Z (1997 and after)
They are also referred to as Zoomers. This Generation are graduating from college right now and they are joining the work force. They are 23 years old. They are the newest and upcoming business owners and entrepreneurs. They are hungry, ambitious, and they are thinking differently from all other generations before them. They want to improve, advance, and do better than their predecessors.

It is important you network and do business with these different generations. They will help you diversify in networking. Your customers and referrals will be coming from all these different generations.

When you network with these generations, you will have huge opportunity to learn from all the different generations. If you are in the older generation and you are not listening to the generations after you then you are missing out. They may be sounding inexperienced especially for the Generation Z but there are areas they may have the best concepts because they see things from a different and recent perspective than you. When you listen to them, you do a lot of good to yourself because they are the future.

They are the future of large, medium, and small-scale business owners and entrepreneurs.

Diversification is the spice of networking, who you network with, how you network and where you network matters a lot. For example, in Accelerated Global Connections (AGC) there are lots of benefits in belonging to AGC. It involves opportunities to share business, build relationships, develop trust, give referrals, and so much more.
One of our proudest achievements of AGC is in its diversity. In terms of gender, we embrace networking with women in

business, the African American Communities, we support Latino businesses and network with the different generations. AGC networks with men and women in the same percentage (50% Men and 50% Women). That is a landmark in networking, AGC is one of the few organizations around the world that can boast of such statistics. We in AGC give equal opportunities to all gender, race, community of people, and the different generations.

"Stop selling and start listening."

Travis Sims

CHAPTER NINETEEN

THE MAGICAL IMPACT OF RELATIONSHIPS IN NETWORKING

It is important and beneficial for you in networking to build solid and quality relationships. Relationships take work on all sides, it requires effort, you have to participate in order to make your relationships great with people. People do not get along in their relationships because they do not put in a lot of work, they do not nurture it. Relationship can help in an era of online communication, especially during a pandemic. You can impact the online presence to bring about growth in relationships which enhances the networks. Do not feel neglected, isolated, or alone, you can be connected and have a great relationship online even during difficult times. You can participate on Zooms, Facebook, Masterminds, and others available to you.

Why Have A Good Relationship?
In order to network effectively, efficiently, and with excellence, you need to have a good relationship. Every great team has excelled in Politics, Military, Sports, Entertainment, Professions etc. because they had a great team. A great team can be built when they have good teamwork. Teamwork is not farfetched; it can only be achieved when there is a good relationship.

Whether it is a Solopreneur, Entrepreneur, or you are just involved in a small business and so on, you will need to connect with others in order to be able to share knowledge, ideas, expertise and so on. This does not only allow you to be a recipient, but it also enables you to be able to be a giver as well.

What Is A Good Relationship?
A Good relationship must carry the following values.

1. Mutual Respect
Every good relationship must start with mutual respect. In starting relationships, you must make sure that you are starting the relationship with someone you already know, you have seen their business, how they show up, follow up, the way it is conducted, you like the way their business is being ran. You might even be connected to them through someone else that you already know, most times in a form of a referral. In the case of a referral, it has to do with someone you respect, trust, and place in high regards. This carries over the credibility of the person who introduced you. Having mutual respect is a great place to start a good relationship. It enables you to be kind and helpful to one another.

2. Mindfulness
Be mindful in keeping each other relevant and in thoughts, keeping each other present in the way you are doing business.

In my relationships, anytime I close a business deal, there is a trigger of thought in me to also think about those in my network. The people I have good relationships with, my most trusted people in my organization. When I have these triggers, all I want to do is to introduce my business associates within my network. I introduce and make referrals on their behalf. That is what it means to be mindful of your network and this can only happen when there are good relationships within your network.

You are always mindful of your network, and this attitude of giving and taking kind of relationship which is mutually beneficial for all those involved. It is not one sided, instead we are helping one another.

3. Welcoming Diversity

To have good relationships in your network, you have to welcome diversity. There is difference in diversity when you talk of race, gender, generations. But if you are only networking with those that think like you, that looks like you then you are missing out from the arrays of opportunities that comes from diversifying your network. You only network up when you diversify. You can grow your business better when you diversify and network with every opportunity that comes your way. Always remember your network is your net worth.

There is a great importance in diversifying your network, because if you want to reach more people outside your industry, people that do not think like you, look like you or do business like you, then you can be able to reach out to them through the relationships that are birthed from the diversity in your network.

I challenge you to look for ways to diversify your network, look for ways to reach out to people with diverse mindsets, diverse ways of doing business with people. Do well to embrace diversity.

4. Open Communication

One of the important things in relationship is to be open to communication. Even if it is something that is difficult to say, I want you to consider open communication in all of your relationships.
In achieving an open communication kind of relationship, you must try within your power to be approachable. Not every CEO, Leader, Business Owners has that level of open communication in their relationships.

I believe that it is important to be open to communication, especially when you are talking about relationships as it pertains to employer and employee, whether it is a family member, a business relationship, or a referral partner that you are able to have an open communication with. You must ensure that you have an open communication always even when it is difficult.

5. Trust
It is the ultimate goal in a relationship. If you are nurturing or building your relationship with friends, families, business partners, no matter what and who it is, trust is the value you should be working to get to. Trust is where you become referable. People will only refer you when they know, like and trust you. In building relationships, trust is the ultimate goal. When people trust you, they are willing to share their business with you, they are ready to refer you to their business partners. They are willing to do things to promote you and this can only happen because of the level of trust they have for you. Trust takes time, do not rush the relationship. People intend to ask for the business way too fast, just slow down, do not rush the trust. People tend to ask for referrals to soon just for their selfish interest even when the level of trust is not even strong enough. Deeper relationships birth trust, it takes time to build trust.

"If you are in Business, an Entrepreneur, you must know that a good relationship is the path to trust, and trust is the path to referral. Referral is the path for more business"

Where To Build A Good Relationship
Relationships can happen anywhere; sometimes I build relationships in the most unusual places like meeting someone in the line of a grocery store. In a hobby situation, for example you like golf, you go out on the golf course, you are hanging out in the golf club or the golf store, these are places where you can build a relationship.

For me it is motorcycling, I also like hiking and where I hike, I meet people there and I start up a conversation. I am never afraid to start up a conversation with anyone. I encourage you to start conversations no matter where you are at. One time while hiking,

I was two hours deep into the north woods of Minnesota near Lake Superior with my wife on a trail. I look up and someone coming from the opposite way says, "Travis Sims is that you?" It turned out to be someone I met while networking professionally.

There are also multi business relationships that are built for you to do networking. So when you attend an event using Accelerated Global Connections (AGC) as an example, whether you are there in-person or you are watching online, you are likely there with people from fifty to about Three hundred people.

I encourage you to start a conversation to get know people. If you are in an in-person event collect a business card or if in an online event, message them afterwards and say:

"I love the motivational talk we attended, what are your thoughts on the topic?"
"I love that portion of our conversation; I would love to dig deeper with you"
"Are you open to meeting with me?"
"Can we set up a zoom or Facebook and jump in one of the messenger rooms?"

I encourage you to build relationships. There are also Chambers of commerce, BNI, Goldstar, Master Networks, B2B, LeTip etc. You can build relationships in all organization such as Rotary, Kiwanis, Lions, Optimist etc. where people want to give back and help others.

These are great places to start relationships. No matter the organization you have been a part of, I personally have been in several ones, you often will join an organization because you see the one hundred people in the room, but you stay in the organization because of the five most fruitful relationships that you have and from there you can expand on it. Most people will stay not because of the one hundred but because of the five most meaningful relationship they have built.

How To Build A Good Working Relationship

A) Develop Your People Skills
This commences simply by starting up a conversation with someone. You show interest by showing up, 80% of life starts by showing up. Be there when your competitors are not there.
Come to any event open-minded, seeking to help others. Come with no expectations rather desire to start a relationship and see where it goes. When you get to an event and you have started a conversation:

- Ask about them
- Learn about them
- Ask some questions about their business
- Ask about how long they have been in business
- Ask about the customers that they serve.
- Ask about their passion
- Ask about what they like to do when they are not working.

There are lots of ways for you to develop your people skills and then take it into a longer conversation.

B) Identify The Kind Of Relationship That You Need
One of the neat things about AGC is their name tags that are given in our in-person events. The name tags are color coded based on the industry. For example, if you like to work with realtors, you can easily go to any in person AGC event, and you can see the realtors and spot them in the room. The same applies with Financial Advisers and all other Careers and Business owners.

You can navigate the room and identify the relationships you want to start with them. This allows you to be strategic and it also helps you to have a laser-focus in on your target market.

Although it is important to identify the kind of market you want to network with, but also understand that many of the referrals that you will get will come from outside that target market, so do not be close minded to other relationships.

C) Schedule Time To Build Relationships
This is something that takes time and a lot of focus to achieve. It is an important part of your regime that you are taking time to build. It could be about attending events, setting so many zoom calls per week, making sure that you are engaged in the networking groups, the masterminds that you are part of, take out time to build relationships.

Be intentional about building a good working relationship. Take the time to set some time in your schedule, so that nothing will be overlooked. You can become so busy with other things and neglect relationship building. Take the time to properly schedule everything that concerns you and it brings about excellence, effectiveness, and efficiency.

D) Appreciate Others
In all the relationships you meet, learn to appreciate others, be thankful for their time. Always be thankful, learn to appreciate the kindness shown by other people. Take out time to make them know that you appreciate them, especially someone who has sent you a referral, it is great to show appreciation with them.

E) Stay Positive
Be positive at all times, it is definitely not easy, but you have to make it your lifestyle. No one likes to network with a negative person. No one wants to network with negative Nelly's or negative Ned's. Always be positive, it is very important.

F) Manage Your Boundaries
You have to compartmentalize your relationships. For example, you may say this is my employer relationship and you may

choose not to socialize with an employee outside of work. For example, if you have a business and your employees becomes your friends, and you hang out with them at work and outside of work. It becomes difficult at times because you cannot fire your friends, you just allow things to slide and that is for detriment of your business and this is not good for business.

Do well to manage your boundaries properly, it is definitely not easy for the open-minded ones, but it also has its merits and demerits, just learn to manage it the right way.

G) Avoid Gossiping
Everyone loves to hear it, and everyone criticizes you for sharing it. So be careful of being the gossip, it never fails, it finds a way to get around to the other person and you end up receiving the confrontation. Avoid being the gossip, it never helps, it carries a lot of negativity around it. Everyone around you worries and fears that they can be the next person, people will be gossiping about anytime they are around you. So, avoid it, it will not help you build a positive supportive relationship.

H) Listen Actively
This is a huge one because most people in a conversation listens to only half of a conversation because they are already thinking about what to reply, what are they going to say next. Learn to listen with both ears, learn to listen intent fully. Learn, pause, and wait before you reply, learn to be a good listener.
People love to talk about their favorite subject, which is always themselves, so let them share. Instead of thinking of ways that you are going to reply, you can reply back with something that was said in the conversation. For example:

- I love how you shared
- This was really of value to me,
- Thank you for sharing with me.

Comment on it before you make the reply, this shows that you are actively listening, and you are engaged in the conversation.

Difficult Relationships

You may have to ask yourself relevant questions regarding this area
-Why do I want to maintain a difficult relationship?
Now some people may be in a difficult relationship because they benefit by getting some form of value. It adds value to them personally and their business. The question that comes to mind is that:

"Are you willingly to live with all other things bothering you in the relationship because of the value this relationship brings to you?"
There will be a time, you will have to evaluate the value of this relationship and if it is worth it. You may decide, "I do not have room for this relationship"

You will just start weaning your way out from the relationship and you will make room for a new relationship. For example, I personally do not have room for negativity. I do not have time to spent on negativity. I do not have time to spend with negative people. I only want to spend quality time with positive and supportive people that have other people's interest at heart. I decide to spend my time with high quality people, so I choose to spend my time with great minds.

I try to remove what I consider difficult relationships because of the negativity that it brings. This does not only apply in business alone but also in family and friendship with others. I have had relationships with long-term friends and family members that I decided to wean away because it was suffocating and sucking out the positivity from me. It was taking the life that was within me, I just could not continue to give in to that energy anymore, I had to let it go.

If you are able to shed away rough and difficult relationships it can make room for great, positive and high-quality relationships. There is a general saying that:

"You are a product of the five people you spend most of your time with" So, in moving forward in your relationships, you have to consider the following:

- Who they are?
- What do you bring to the table?
- What do they bring to the table?

Relationships are very important in creating your business and doing it the right way. I encourage you to really focus on the following:

- The relationships that you are building.
- How you are building them
- Where you are building them
- The time you are putting into the relationships.
- Consider the foundation you have built in your relationships.

"Accountability is the secret sauce to success."

Travis Sims

CHAPTER TWENTY

ACCOUNTABILITY; THE SECRET OF SUCCESS IN NETWORKING

Accountability is a situation in which someone is responsible for things that happens and can give a satisfactory reason for them.
As a person interested in having success in networking, you must be accountable. You must be accountable so that to create good relationships and have great networks. In delivering success in networking, accountability is the vehicle that takes you to the destination. It helps us to deliver success because success comes from accountability.

Accountability has to do with values, morals, integrity, responsibility, diligence, discipline, trust, relationships, greatness, being honorable and ethical. When you are accountable, you are held at higher standards, you are respected by people.

Accountability creates loyalty, honesty, and trust, and these are really difficult to come by but with accountability it is achievable. It is a key ingredient within your network, business, and teams that you are participating in.

"Leadership is about taking responsibility and not making excuses."

Accountability Starts With You
Leadership defines the culture, as a leader you must hold yourself accountable. Holding yourself accountable is creating a higher standard for yourself. You can hold yourself accountable in multiple areas.

For example, I hold myself accountable that:

- I will get up early every morning.
- I will focus on my attitude of gratitude.
- I will review my goals
- I will create my work list for the day.
- I will do my exercise.
- I will maintain my nutrition.
- I will make my spouse feel valued, make her understand how important she is to me.
- I will support the goals of my Spouse.
- I will help my team and help them grow.
- I will give my team the essence from the value they derive in participating in the AGC.

These are some of the things I am accountable for, you can write yours. Every goal driven and successful person I have come across have the things they are accountable for and they do them excellently.

You Are Accountable
Accountability shows great qualities in leadership, as a leader you must be accountable. You must be accountable to your success or your failures, this fact is very important. As a leader you do not only take responsibility for the successes but also for the failures as well.
People will come to lose confidence in you when you have this attitude of accumulating the successes and pushing the failures to every other person apart from you. When something goes wrong most people find a way to push the blame to someone else. The human nature likes to point the blame in the direction of someone else.

They use statements such as:

- It is because of what they did.
- It is because I was doing my part and the team was not doing theirs.
- I did my part and they did not do their part that is why we failed, is all their fault.

Humans have the nature of wanting to blame everyone else apart from themselves. As a leader who is networking you must take the responsibility of accountability whether in success or in failure. If we fail to measure up in any of those capacities, it is my fault.

People tend to respect those who are accountable for their actions even in failures, especially when things do not work out. Accountability is admitting the situation even when things go bad. Admit that you are wrong, learn from what happened and move forward.

Accountability Is Not A One Time Thing
Accountability is not a one-time thing, but it is an all-time thing. You have to hold yourself accountable all the time to all the things you said you will do. What makes you referable in that you show up when you say you will, and you will follow up when you say will follow up. When you do not show up or do not follow up to the referrals you have been sent. People connected to you in your network will be less likely to refer you in the future.

It takes a long time to earn trust, but it takes a really short time to lose it. Accountability is what makes you trustworthy. If you agree to do something, do it at the right time and in the right way.

You must make accountability an all-time thing and it is not a one-time thing.

Accountability Applies To One And To All

If you are leading a team environment, accountability applies to everyone on the team, you should not play favorites. It is quite natural to find your favorite people, work with your favorite person, it is natural to have friends who you like in that environment. However, you have to hold friends and family accountable to the same standard that you set for everyone else.

I had to learn about accountability at a very young age. This happened because I grew up in my Dad's business, he taught me about accountability and held me in even a higher standard than anyone else on the team. He did not play favorites with me, neither did he just allow me to get away with everything and held everyone accountable for it instead. He held me to even a higher standard than everyone else in the group of people working for him. At first, I did not understand because I was very young and naive because he was always pushing me harder than everyone else. He made me to understand that even as his son, he expected more from me. He expects me to stand up and be a leader in my own rank. He taught me this great lesson of accountability at a very early age, and this has been instrumental to my success.

The central lesson in my story is that if you have friends and families working with you, they must be held accountable to the same standard as everyone else on the team. Do not allow others to be accountable in a higher standard and allow the others to slip below it. You have to have a team dynamic that applies to all.

Accountability Can Not Be Delegated

People have to sign up for accountability, they have to own their accountability, it simply means you have to ask for their permission.

Imagine a sport without rules, that can be a terrible sight. Imagine if no one kept score, will you sign up and play in it? I will not want to play in a sport if I do not know the rules. It is the same principle that applies in networking and business. In networking for example people want to know the rules before signing up. They want to know all that the group or organization is all about before signing up. You cannot hold me accountable when I do not know what the rules are, that is why I must know the rules before signing up for it.

You must explain the rules upfront, for example in this networking group, I expect you to:

- Show up on time for meetings
- Participate in the activities.
- Follow up with the referrals that you have received.
- Track your results.
- Is it ok if I hold you accountable to the rules of the groups or to the dynamics of the organization?

For example, in Accelerated Global Connections (AGC), in our mastermind group, the persons in my network said yes to the rules before we integrated them into our network. I got the permission to keep them accountable. This is very important because if you do not have their permission, people will always say:

"Why are you hounding me with this, I did not sign up for this."
So, it is important that you must get their permission. Accountability can never be delegated; they have to say yes to it. It is a very important variable in networking especially when working with a team of people.

People are humans and humans make mistakes, but they must approve, they must say it is ok and give you their permission before you can hold them accountable for it.

Accountability Is The Difference Between Success And Failure

This is true because if you have a group of people that you do not hold accountable, let say you are working with the team or in a group dynamic and you just leave them to their own account.

-You did not ask them if they are following through.
- You did not ask them if they are putting in the work.
-You did not ask them if they did what they said they were going to do.

Now if you do not hold them to that standard, suddenly your group of accountable people will now become a group of spectators. Let me give you a solid example that will drive this home perfectly. Let us show an example with sports, the people that are running up and down the court, running up and down the field, skating up and down the ice, they are always making more money than those sitting on the bench. This is because they showed up in practice, they held themselves accountable for putting in their best during practice. In practice they aspired for excellence, efficiency, and effectiveness.

They gained the support needed, they became active, engaged participants and members of the team. The moment you do not hold them accountable, they become spectators and spectators just sit and watch things happen, they go out in the stands and often cast blame especially when the team is not playing well.

The fans in the stands show their support and cheer the team on with everything they have when the team is excelling but when the team is losing, the same people are the ones casting the blame, they are the first to say the team sucks, they demand the sack of the coach and lots more. They are the ones with all the opinions because they are spectators, they are not participants, they are not accountable to the team because they are not the players who are making the most money.

Accountability can be the difference between your success and your failures in all the group dynamics that you are participating in. It is important that you hold your team accountable. You must keep them in engaging in all activities.

You Must Hold People Accountable

You can achieve this by signing up for review sessions. Remember that accountability is not a one-time thing, and it applies to everyone. You have to place your rules on accountability. You must inform them and ask them:

"Can I hold you accountable for these things?"

To hold people accountable, you are to bring those sheets that they signed, this is why I have contracts. It is a definition of what is expected. It is a list of expectations that someone signs up for and agrees on. This could be in an email format, it could be on your website, it could also be in a form of contract that both parties have signed. It is what is written that you can hold a person accountable for.

To hold anyone accountable is to go back and review:

- What was agreed upon.
- What did we say we will do.
- What did we say we will follow up on.

Both parties will meet each other's expectations, both parties can hold each other accountable to the agreement and expectations. Accountability is important in getting clarity and understanding. You can only hold anyone accountable when you have the rules to the game. Do well to review them regularly.

I will regularly ask a question like:

"Where do you think we fell short on our agreement?"

You will just sit back and listen to the conversation. It is not a yes or no question and answer, but it is a conversational question, meaning it gives them the opportunity to participate in the conversation. It gives you the opportunity to listen to what others have to say. You always have to listen to what others have to say. Always remember that people like to make excuses, so you must ask these questions:

- Is it ok to hold you in a higher standard?
- Is it ok if you are held with the standard that you agreed upon?
- Is it ok if I do not allow you to make excuses?

If they say yes to all these questions, they are giving you the permission to hold them accountable.
Do not make excuses, do not blame it on things such as COVID-19, The Economy, The Government and so on, eradicate those excuses that are keeping you from achieving your goals. You have to pick yourself up, adjust, adapt, and hold yourself accountable to the success you have planned to achieve. You can hear excuses about the current climate of business, that a recession is looming on the way, but you have to disregard such excuses, focus on the goal and hold yourself accountable for it like no one else.

The questions to be answered are to show if you are accountable in your network:

- Are you showing up?
- Are you engaging in your network?
- Are you asking for referrals?
- Are you clear with those referrals?

- Are you setting up one on one meetings?
- Are you setting up face to face appointments?
- Are you making excuses?

You cannot make money and excuses, you will have to choose to go out and make more money and accountability is the key.

AFTERWORDS

Networking has come to stay and is even more essential in the modern world than ever before. With all the great benefits you have come to know going through these pages, its importance is similar to oxygen to humans as Networking is to Business owners, Entrepreneurs and other Professionals. Every one of these categories must be Networking if they want to be successful and make an impact in their business and careers.

The most successful people in the world understand that it is not what you know, it is about who you know and how well they know you that counts. They understand that their network is their net worth, so they place premium on it to invest hugely in their network. They invest time, trust, relationships, and so much more.

Many people have been told to go out and do networking, to grow your business, or advance your career. However, networking is not taught in college and most people have no idea how to network effectively. Just like magic is a learned and honed skill of the magician. Networking is a skill that must be learned and mastered.

Networking is not the question for the businessmen or women and professionals, networking is the answer, and this answer is never wrong. Networking is now a culture, it is a way of life of people, namely; Business Owners, Entrepreneurs, other Professionals. Anyone that wants to leave a mark in their career or business must make networking their go-to-place. When you are able to network successfully you enjoy the magical experience of Networking.

There is a lot of benefits in networking as we read through the pages of the book, because it has to be done excellently, efficiently and effectively. It is not breaking news that the most connected people are the most successful people; you can see that the success trail goes all the way back to networking. As the principles and core values are upheld it will help you to improve on your skill set and stay on course in your career. Networking helps to bring about career development, it helps businesspeople to keep in touch with opportunities and helps Professionals keep pulse in the job market.

You have seen behind the curtain some of the biggest networking secrets that only the elite have discovered. You have learned how to effectively build relationships, gain trust, develop referrals and close more business while being authentically yourself.

By using the principles taught within this book, networking done effectively, efficiently, and excellently will propel you to the peak of your business and career.

"The highest compliment you can give a Business Owner or Salesperson is an introduction to your network."

Travis Sims.

ABOUT THE AUTHOR

Travis Sims is a Networking Expert, Motivational Speaker, and Thought Leader committed to helping you become a better person, leader, and networker. Travis is a powerful Keynote Speaker engaging audience as large as 3,000 people from all over the world in 49 different countries. For 15 years Travis was a high-level executive for a global business networking organization breaking records of achievement nationally and internationally.

Travis is known worldwide as the Magician of Networking. He has been teaching & coaching the best business leadership minds across the country how to do networking, build networks, and create community. Travis is the CEO of AGC Accelerated Global Connections. He is on a mission to help accelerate local business connections in social settings around the world that foster relationships resulting in global opportunities. Travis is an Amazon #1 Best Selling Author with his book "Networking In The New Normal." Teaching business professionals how to grow & thrive during and beyond Covid-19.

In 2013, Travis set a goal to lose 100 pounds in one year. He not only accomplished this goal, but he has kept the weight off. Travis has completed some of the toughest competitive Mud Obstacle Courses on the planet, running in the following races: Warrior Dash, Rugged Maniac, Spartan, Battle Frog and the Tough Mudder. Travis enjoys Kickboxing and Martial Arts. He recently earned his blue belt in Kempo Karate.

Travis believes his success can be attributed to setting goals reviewing them regularly and a strong desire to accomplish them.

www.ingramcontent.com/pod-product-compliance
Lightning Source LLC
Chambersburg PA
CBHW020649220526
45464CB00001B/353